What people are saying about this book:

"I like this book because the information is well presented and consistent. It will be useful to both hunters and field trialers. Field trial training is a logical extension of a well-trained hunting dog. Both types of training are based on obedience and rapport with your dog."

—Ron Zook, President, American Brittany Club, OH

"This manual states simply how to train a bird dog without cruelty. It delineates a comprehensive step-by-step procedure to humanely train a bird dog. It will school him from pre-elementary to college-level status. The methods Dave uses and teaches in his seminars, videos, and this book are more humane and practical than the methods described in other well-known dog training books I have read."

—Sue D'Arcy, Field Trialer and Brittany Breeder, NM

"The directions and tips in Walker's book are informative and easily understood. Throughout the book you can feel his deep love for dogs."

—T. J. Sullivan, M.D., ID

"I like this book. It has clear step-by-step instructions that a novice can follow. I found greater and better step-by-step details in this book than in other well-known dog training books I've read. This book makes me yearn to begin again with a puppy. Its contents appeal to both hunters and field trial amateurs because the route to producing a good hunting dog and producing a good field trial dog is basically the same."

—Dr. David Kenney,
Professor Emeritus, Southern Illinois University
and former Director of the Illinois Department of Conservation

"I have a new pup, and I plan to train him as close to Walker's training methods as I can."

—Dale Boll, Potato Farmer, Hunter, ID

"The strength of this book is the sound advice it contains and the easy-to-follow instructions. The approach is simple, and everyone can use it. It will be a fine addition to any dog handler's bookshelf."
—*Harve Thorn, Educator, Handler, and Trainer, AR*

"Walker's excellent book can be used to train dogs from house pets to champion field trial dogs."
—*Ken Kloepfer, Attorney-at-Law, Retired Judge, CA*

"I like what Walker says and the way he says it. This manual is a bird dog trainer's bible. You can train dogs by it."
—*James B. Buchanan, Veteran Hunter and Trainer, OH*

"This book contains lots of information, stresses respect for dogs, and with it good dog training can be done."
—*Jeannette Casenave, Playwright, CA*

"The clear, concise, and to-the-point instructions in this manual will be of great benefit to both field trialers and hunters."
—*George E. Walker, Retired Supervisor, Dept. of Labor, OSHA*

"The kindness of the training and the way it all ties together are major strengths of Dave's book. It explains every phase of dog training a person would ever want."
—*Jerry Jordan, Kojac Kennels, Inc., IA*

"As an exhibitor of purebred dogs, a few years ago I decided to train my dogs for hunting and field trialing. While attending a well-known dog training seminar, I asked about field trialing and was told, 'Just do it.' The seminar information was not commensurate with the cost. When I met Fay and Dave, they willingly shared their vast training expertise with me. Of all the dog books I've read, Dave's book is the only one that covers all phases of training— puppy to champion. It is excellent, and the emphasis on the correct use of the e-collar is one of its strongest parts."
—*Charles H. Smith II, Senopah Kennel, TX*

The
BIRD DOG
TRAINING MANUAL

How to Make Your Dog a
Great Hunter or a
Field Trial Champion

Dave Walker

Wade & Moeur Publishing, LLC • Ontario, Oregon

The Bird Dog Training Manual

How to Make Your Dog a Great Hunter or a Field Trial Champion

by Dave Walker

Published by
Wade & Moeur Publishing, LLC
P. O. Box 623
Ontario, Oregon 97914
www.wadeandmoeur.com

ISBN, printed ed. 0-9764617-0-6

Library of Congress Cataloging-in-Publication Data

Walker, Dave
The bird dog training manual: how to make your dog a great hunter or a field trial champion
Includes index.

Dedication
To Fay

My wife, my partner, my friend, the love of my life.

CONTENTS

Foreword by Bill West

Dave Walker's book *The Bird Dog Training Manual* is unparalleled. If you want to train your dog yourself, use this book. It is thorough, practical, easily understood, contains a plethora of explanatory pictures, and you can use it to train your bird dog.

There are dog trainers, and there are dog training books. I've known Dave for over 25 years, and, without a doubt, he is one of the best bird dog trainers in the country. I've been working with dogs—training, handling, hunting, judging, teaching, and helping other trainers, including Dave—for over 50 years, and this is the best bird dog training book I've ever seen.

I might add that of all the trainers I've worked with, Dave is one of the most enthusiastic and apt trainers. Dog training is an art that takes patience and perseverance. In this book, Dave clearly lays out in a step-by-step process how to train your dog for your needs and desires—always stressing the importance of patience and perseverance. He shares his years of accumulated professional knowledge gained through experience, acute observation of dogs, and working with other professionals. Dave has developed a unique way of training dogs. It is simple. It is straightforward. It works. His dogs are happy dogs that look good around their game.

Dave and I share a similar philosophy. Basic to our philosophy is the tenet that you don't have to be cruel to a dog to train him. Dogs are loving, social animals. No one knows this better than Dave.

Like so many of us who've been in the dog training business longer than we care to admit, he began training his own dogs when he was a kid. The watchword of the bird dog training world then was cruelty. Harsh training was part of the old school trainers' belief that a dog raised in the house couldn't be a good hunting dog. Dave has proved over and over that you can accomplish more with kindness than you can with cruelty and that a dog can be a family pet, a faithful buddy in the field, and a superb hunter or field trial champion.

By using Dave's training methods that are clearly and concisely discussed in his book—*The Bird Dog Training Manual*—you'll not only be able to train your dog, you'll develop a rewarding and productive relationship with man's best friend.

—Bill West

Preface—Note to the Reader

"In order to really enjoy a dog, one doesn't merely try to train him to be semi-human. The point of it is to open oneself to the possibility of becoming partly a dog."

—Edward Hoagland

Dog training is an art, not a science. Good bird dog training is like a piece of fabric. It is seamless—not separate pieces stitched together. No one part is separate from the other parts. Many a good dog has been ruined because a trainer tried to teach one thing at a time.

This book is an effort to explain simply, straightforwardly, and honestly the most humane and effective way to train dogs. I'm neither withholding tricks of the trade nor suggesting any procedures or tactics that haven't been tested and re-tested—often through countless trial and error sessions with dogs.

My intent is to share my love of dogs and my dog training experiences with people who love their dogs and want them to become the best they can be. It's my earnest hope that this manual will help people become better dog owners, better dog handlers, and better dog trainers—maximizing the pleasure of the relationship between a person and a dog.

When I was a boy, my father began teaching me to hunt. While learning to hunt, I became interested in training dogs. I wasn't particular about what kind of dogs I had, as long as I had dogs to train and to hunt. I had black and tan hounds, beagles, pointers, setters, and several "Heinz 57" mixed breeds and valued all for their particular abilities.

When I started training dogs, I watched and listened to local trainers who were using traditional methods. They powdered a dog's behind with bird shot if he flushed or chased birds. If he blinked birds, they took him on a one-way hunting trip. They twisted his ears or toes for disobedience. They stepped on his foot to teach him to give up a retrieved bird. It didn't take long for me to figure out that cruelty and harshness were key components in their training.

As I studied the training techniques of the day, I decided there must be a more effective and more humane way.

Dogs—like children—want to please, but to do so they must first be taught what pleases and what doesn't. At that time I started experimenting with different techniques—specifically concentrating on combining training components with dog walking.

Cruelty or inhumane treatment plays no part in my training. Dogs cannot learn when they're hurting or feeling they're being hurt either by your actions or the tone of your voice.

In the early '60s I began experimenting with the electronic collar, commonly called an e-collar. When an e-collar is used correctly, it doesn't hurt a dog; it spooks him. I had already found that I needed to put a collar on dogs so I could use the collar to shake or *spin* (lifting a dog's forefeet off the ground and rotating him 360 degrees) him for correction. I was looking for something—I wasn't sure what—to use with the e-collar to reduce its spooking effect.

Retiring from the U. S. Navy in 1973, I devoted all of my time to working with dogs and developing my training techniques. I was still searching for something to use with the e-collar. When I saw a training collar in a magazine, I ordered it because I thought it could be used to spin a dog and it might be something that could be used with the e-collar.

Training with Bill West, I noticed he was using a training collar similar to the one I had, but his was better. Using those as prototypes, I began modifying them and eventually came up with my version of a *no hurt* training collar. This collar is more humane and is equally effective as other training collars. Through the years I've made and sold hundreds of my *Dave Walker™* training collars. *See* **Appendix 4 – Useful Names and Addresses**.

Continuing to experiment, I found that by using a check-cord attached to the training collar, I could flip the check-cord to make a popping sound with the buckle connecting the training collar and check-cord. The sound got the dog's attention, but it didn't spook him. Through trial and error, I learned the spooking effect of the e-collar could be mitigated by simultaneously combining the shaking of the collar, the feel of the e-collar, and the popping sound of the training collar buckle.

I began training with the dog wearing both the e-collar and the training collar. At first I used just the check-cord and training collar—not the e-collar—to get a dog's attention. When a dog began to respond consistently to the stimulation of the check-cord and training collar—after many training sessions—I combined the stimulation of the e-collar with the training-collar stimulation. The dog did not separate the stimuli. I never use the e-collar alone until all field work is completed.

The principle of my training is akin to associative learning—learning that is based on the belief that ideas and experiences reinforce one another and can be mentally linked to enhance the learning process.

Through the years I've developed a way of training bird dogs, using the e-collar in all phases of it—not to hurt the dog but to enhance both speed of learning and retention. I use it as a training device as well as a correction device. A dog can learn from fear, but fear spoils the great relationship of a hunting team: companions in the field enjoying and pleasing each other. The results of my years of experimental training have become known as *Walker's Way*. My method is simple: walk a dog in a prescribed manner and simultaneously teach verbal and nonverbal commands.

To have a dog you enjoy and are proud of, train him logically, treat him humanely, and consider his needs and wants.

My dog training is not compatible with the practices and procedures of most other dog trainers. If you're going to use my way, do not use potentially harmful or confusing gadgets, devices, or techniques such as choke chains, whoa posts, barrels, pinch collars (also called spike collars), half-hitches around a dog's belly, poles, bird launchers, dizzied birds under bushes, knots in check-cords, and so forth. These have no place in my training. When people want to know if I use any gadgetry, I tell them, "No, I can't carry those along on my back when I'm training or hunting in the field."

If you do not have a check-cord, training collar, and electronic collar, or are not comfortable using them, you can still use my method of dog training. You will need some kind of lead—one no more than 12 feet long—which you attach to your dog's ID collar. You must not talk to your dog except to teach explicit verbal performance commands. Follow the same procedures given in this manual: walking, flipping the lead, shaking or spinning the dog for correction, never letting him pull on the lead, and petting him when he makes proper responses. This training (without a training collar and an electronic collar) takes much longer, and the retention rate is not as great. It's a matter of personal preference, the amount of time you devote to the training, and the extent of training you want your dog to have.

The art of walking a dog while teaching all the commands is central to my training. This training is done through mental and physical strategies and positive reinforcement, rather than through physical practices that may cause pain, fear, or confusion. Your dog will respond to this type of training. Praise through petting brings pleasure to your dog and makes him want to please you by responding to both verbal and nonverbal commands.

Repetition and consistency are essential. The training is not linear; it is cyclic. Training is not like putting nuts on bolts. All too often trainers think that once they've taught a procedure it's permanent. Such is not the case. You must constantly go over previously learned experiences as you introduce new ones. Just as children learn, dogs learn by constant and consistent reinforcement. Be consistent and work with your dog every day if possible. He will retain the information longer. In education this is called carryover. The more intense the training the more carryover you will get, and you will have to spend less time repeating elements of the training.

This training is highly effective and can be used to train very young dogs because it doesn't frighten or hurt them. It can be initiated much earlier than other types, and dogs retain it much longer.

By using this manual, you can train your dog to be your best buddy—one you can be proud of as a hunter or field trial champion.

—Dave Walker

For ease in writing, the word *dog* in this manual refers to both sexes.

Acknowledgments

Scores of people contributed suggestions for this book, and I thank them.

First, I am grateful to the reviewers who read the first draft of the manuscript and made numerous valuable suggestions for improvements: George Walker, AL; Bill West, TX; David A. Webb, PA; Dr. T. J. Sullivan, ID; June McConnell, ID; Maurice Lindley, SC; Dr. David Kenney, IL; Jerry Jordan, IA; Hank Hartnek, AZ; Sue D'Arcy, NM; Dale R. Boll, ID; James B. Buchanan, OH; Robert Akers, CA.

I especially want to thank Fred Brune, WA; Jeannette Casenave, CA; Martha H. Greenlee, VA; Ken Kloepfer, CA; Charles H. "Buster" Smith, TX; and Harve Thorn, AR for reading the first draft and subsequent revisions, always making useful contributions to the improvement of the book.

Special thanks go to Ronald L. Bohuslov for book design and photography, Fay Walker for jacket photo and others, Barry Arthur for the title page painting, and Teresa S. Sales of Caxton Printers for cover design.

Finally, I thank Esther Buchanan for copyediting and for her patient, professional guidance in helping me translate my years of experience into a form I can share with dog owners who want to train their dogs effectively and humanely.

About the Author

Born in rural Alabama during the Great Depression, early in life Dave learned the value of good bird dogs. In 1952 he joined the U. S. Navy and saw active duty during the Korean conflict. He spent most of the first half of his naval career aboard ships; the last half he was a recruiter and an instructor for the U. S. Naval Reserve. Preparing lesson plans and lecturing was his career, but bird dog training was his passion. During these years, he began to professionally train dogs on a part-time basis.

When he retired from the Navy in 1973, he secured a VA loan, built a dog kennel, and began training dogs full time.

Through the years Dave has trained hundreds of dogs and helped countless dog owners and handlers become better dog people. As the old saying goes, "The proof of the pudding is in the eating," and Dave's method has proven its worth. The dogs he's trained and helped others train are what he calls *good citizens*—well-trained dogs. They do what they're supposed to do—hunting or field trialing— and are a joy to their owners. He has always shared his knowledge and expertise with anyone who asks for help.

Friends and fellow dog lovers prevailed upon Dave to begin giving training seminars, which he has since conducted in Idaho, Iowa, Massachusetts, Missouri, North Dakota, Pennsylvania, South Carolina, Texas, and in several provinces of Canada. People attending these seminars asked him to film his techniques. In response to their requests, he developed a series of dog training videos. *See* **Appendix 4 – Useful Names and Addresses**. Dog trainers and dog owners continue to call Dave to thank him for these tapes and to tell him how useful they are in both training dogs and correcting behavior problems.

People have repeatedly asked Dave when he was going to write a book. His reply has always been that he would write it when he had time. Finally, he decided he would just have to take the time to turn his years of experience into black marks on paper. Dog owners, trainers, and handlers now have this complete, systematic explanation of how to train bird dogs for hunting and/or for field trialing.

When Dave and his wife Fay—who teaches obedience and conformation classes and shows dogs—are not on the field trial campaign road, they're at home in the beautiful rolling hills of southwest Idaho where they help dogs become better bird dogs and dog owners become better handlers. Walker's Plantation and Kennel is never without guests— dogs to be trained and eager people to be taught.

CHAPTER 1

CHOOSING YOUR DOG

Assessing Your Needs
Expectations
Considering Your Environment
Classifying Dogs

Choosing your dog is a very personal matter, and many variables will enter into your decision. Your reason for getting a bird dog, where you live—the part of the country, apartment, house, city, town, country, and so forth—and your personality and temperament will play a role in your decision. If you're looking for a long-term, rewarding experience with the animal that's come to be known as "man's best friend," carefully consider the breed and the bloodlines of your prospective dog.

Breed

When you're considering the breed you want, logically, the key elements you should consider are form and function, for in dogs, as in art, the form follows the function. Consider your reason for getting a dog. Do you want a hunting companion? If so, what type of hunting will you be doing? Where will you be hunting? What type of terrain and weather will be involved? Do you intend to field trial your dog? If so, what class interests you—gun dog or all age dog?

Consider your own personality and temperament. If you are mild-mannered, patient, and quiet, a sensitive dog might be a better choice for you than one that requires more aggressive handling. If you are an aggressive, outgoing, strong-minded person, and perhaps a little short on patience, you might want a dog that requires a firmer but not abusive hand.

Breeds are divided into the following seven groups: Sporting Dogs, Hounds, Working Dogs, Terriers, Toy Dogs, Non-sporting Dogs, and Herding Dogs.

Bird dogs belong to the sporting dog group. Bird dogs are bred for pointing, flushing, and retrieving. Some excel in only one area; some excel in two; and some excel in all three.

Selecting your dog logically sounds good, but the truth of the matter is that most people don't choose dogs logically. They choose them emotionally based on past experiences. They may choose a breed they had as a child, one that their father or mother owned, one owned by a favorite uncle or aunt, one owned by a grandparent, or even a friend. There is nothing wrong with choosing a breed based on pleasant past experiences. Dog ownership should be pleasant and emotionally rewarding.

Bloodlines

Now that you've decided on the breed, you need to consider the bloodlines (direct line of descent—pedigree). Choosing the specific dog that's right for you from a particular line is just as important as choosing the breed. Choosing bloodlines may be a little more logical than choosing the breed, but you'll ask some of the same questions. If you want a big-running field trial dog, choose a line that consistently produces big-running dogs. If you want a field trial gun dog, choose a line that consistently produces good gun dogs. If you are a hunter, choose the bloodline that consistently produces good hunting dogs. The line doesn't always guarantee that you'll get what you want, but it will improve the odds.

Breeder

Find a good breeder. Check the web sites devoted to the breed of your choice. Check with local breed clubs and/or the American Kennel Club (AKC). Talk with veterinarians, groomers, and owners of dogs of the breed you want. These people usually know the names of reputable breeders in your area. Visit as many of these breeders as possible before you get your puppy. Be wary of breeders who seem to be trying to make a hard sell. Does the breeder impress you as being honest, open, and informative? Does the breeder have a satisfaction policy? Some reputable breeders guarantee only the health condition. Others guarantee not only the health of the dog but will replace him or refund the money if a client for any reason is dissatisfied with the dog. Look for a breeder who stands behind his dogs.

Picking a Pup

After you've decided on the breed, the bloodline, and the breeder that will give you a dog that will meet your needs, you come to the exciting and often nerve-wracking decision of choosing a particular pup.

There are probably as many ways to pick the right pup as there are people picking them. Some people watch a litter of pups and choose the one that is the most aggressive— one more interested in exploring than eating. Some people look for a pup that's already showing dominant characteristics.

When I choose a pup, I first consider the breed and then the bloodline offering what I want in a particular dog. The dogs I choose must come from a line I like, and they must have good trainability characteristics in their pedigree. I pick field trial champion bred pups because they are more trainable and can be trained at a younger age.

Brittany pups: Pick me, pick me.

Choosing a pup that demonstrates boldness (assertiveness and dominance) is certainly a good way to select a particular pup. My favorite way of picking a pup is to go into the kennel with the puppies, close my eyes, hold out my hand, and the pup that jumps up to smell my hand gets my attention. A dog that will jump up to smell a strange hand is demonstrating not only his boldness but also his scenting ability—good nose. Since I'm partial to good looking dogs, I open my eyes, pick up the pup, and, if he has markings that appeal to me, he's my pick of the litter.

Choosing Older Dog or Pup

When you get a pup, you've got a great deal of work ahead and more than a few headaches, including training him and making sure he stays healthy. An older dog probably has had quite a bit of training and has survived the puppyhood health problems. Although the cost of an older dog is considerably more, it may be worth it. Training and health care translate into time and money. On the other hand, most people can't resist picking their pup and going through the enjoyable but often frustrating puppy phase. It's your choice. There are pros and cons on both sides.

Classifying Dogs

Classifying dogs according to maturity is useful in understanding training phases. Dogs, like children, go through specific maturation periods—childhood to adolescence to maturity. Roughly, dog training phases may be put into these three categories: the puppy phase, the adolescent phase, and the mature dog phase. These phases should not be thought of in terms of chronological (calendar) ages, but rather in terms of mental and/or ability ages based on the extent of the training they've received and have retained. For example, some six-month old puppies may be as broke as some mature dogs. Dogs—like people—mature in different ways at different rates, and the type of training a young dog receives affects his maturation process.

Puppy Phase

In the puppy phase you can start teaching your pup a few manners, such as *stand-up-stand-still*—if you're sufficiently gentle. The younger your pup is the more likely he'll dislike this training. This is particularly true if you're harsh or he doesn't understand what's happening. You can do a lot of training when your pup is quite young if you do it the right way: Following the instructions in this manual. Patience and gentleness are essential.

Adolescent Phase

Think about what you want from your dog. Do you want a great hunting companion, or do you want a great field trial champion? To a certain extent, the dog's purpose determines the training during adolescence.

Always train him for his purpose first. After he's mastered this training, then you may teach him obedience commands such as *SIT* and *HEEL* or trick commands such as *ROLL OVER, BEG*, and *SHAKE*.

Be aware that teaching him obedience or trick commands before he is solid on his hunting commands and is a seasoned dog in the field may interfere with his hunting. If you teach your dog to *SIT* before he is a seasoned dog, he may sit when he is pointing. This, of course, is not a good thing for a pointing dog. You want your dog to look good when he's on point, whether he's hunting or competing.

The American Kennel Club (AKC) uses the term *derby dog* to classify an adolescent dog that is at least 6 months old, but not older than 24 months. This term is meaningless to hunters since it is used only for dogs competing in field trials. If an adolescent dog is going to do field trial work, he needs to be able to run as big as you want him to run before you start serious training of any type that will result in a mature, finished dog. This includes obedience and discipline.

Depending upon the dog and the type of training that is done, a dog classified as a *derby dog* may be able to run as a mature, polished dog. For example, Dual Champion Shady's Tia Maria, a Brittany bitch, was a mature dog— trained and broke as a field champion—at an extremely young calendar age. She was the number one all-age Brittany bitch in the nation and became a dual champion at a very young age. According to *The Brittany Magazine*, she was the youngest dual dog in history to compete in the American Brittany Club (ABC) Nationals as a dual champion. Field champion Chubasco—finished at 16 months—was the youngest field champion to compete in the ABC Nationals.

Mature Dog Phase

Dog's, like people's, developmental and physical ages are not always consistent with calendar age. Using the training described in this manual, some dogs may reach a high level of maturity at a young age. The time it takes to reach this level of maturity depends upon the training and basic personality of the particular dog.

A great deal of the training done for both the mature hunting dog and the mature field trial dog is identical. Generally, field trial dogs should run as big (range out) as far as their handler wants them to run before they are broke.

You may begin training your dog earlier if you're going to use him solely for hunting, because you don't have to be guided by the requirements of AKC for field trial dogs. First, train your dog for work he'll be doing. A hunting dog may be fully trained by the time he's six months old.

As you get to know your dog in the adolescent phase, you must decide on what you want him to be able to do as a well-trained adult dog. Will you use him for personal bird hunting trips with friends for your own enjoyment? Will you enter him in competition? If you want a well-trained bird dog you must learn the vocabulary of terms for different skill levels good bird dogs have.

Skill 1:
Dog trained to be *steady-to-wing*

You release your dog in the field. He locates a bird, freezes, and points at the area where the bird is (visible or hidden in cover). He *stands-up-stands-still* in the pointing stance and holds this position while you catch up with him, pass him, go toward the bird until the bird *flushes* (flies away). So a dog trained to be *steady-to-wing* stays put in the pointing stance *(stands-up-stands-still)* and waits while you flush the bird. He does not run after a flushed bird. He *holds point* while you walk past him. You reward him by petting him.

The final test of whether your dog is *steady-to-wing* is that he does not move when you flush birds away from him, back over him, or in any direction. He stands and points, even if he sees a bird that is running. He *holds point* until you silently go to him and release him with a nonverbal command.

After your dog is perfectly reliable on *steady-to-wing*, you will probably want to take him to the next level—*steady-to-wing-and-shot*.

Skill 2:
Dog trained to be *steady-to-wing-and-shot*

If your dog is *steady-to-wing*, he is a hunting dog, but most hunters want their dogs trained to be *steady-to-wing-and-shot*. With careful training and conditioning, he does not fear the noise of a gun being shot at birds flushed in front of him. He trusts you and *holds point* when birds flush or run away from him and when you shoot them.

When your dog has become reliable at (1) finding and pointing birds and *holding point* after you flush them, and (2) still *holds point* while you shoot a shotgun in front of him at birds flying away from him, you may start training him at the next level—*steady-to-wing-shot-and-kill.*

Skill 3:
Dog trained to be *steady-to-wing-shot-and-kill*

In being *steady-to-wing-shot-and-kill*, your dog *holds point* and *stands-up-and-stands-still* while you shoot the bird and remains standing while you get the bird and bring it back to him. This procedure is accomplished in silence, except for the report of the gun. You give no verbal commands. Your dog knows to stay put.

After a dog is (1) *steady-to-wing* (*holds point* when birds are flushed), (2) is *steady-to-wing-and-shot* (*holds point* when birds are flushed and gun is fired), and is (3) *steady-to-wing-shot-and-kill* (*holds point* when birds are flushed, gun is fired, and you retrieve the birds), some hunters want their dog to move to the next level—*retrieving-on-command.*

Skill 4:
Dog trained to *retrieve-on-command*

Your dog goes on point, is steady throughout the *wing-shot-and-kill* sequence. You release him from *holding point* by giving him a verbal command—whatever word you use to let him know you want him to go get the bird. He goes to the bird, picks it up, returns to you, holds the bird until you give him the verbal command GIVE, and he then places the bird in your hand.

Some handlers use the word *fetch* to let their dog know they want him to get the bird; however, many handlers use the dog's name. Calling his name works fine. If another dog or dogs are honoring, they may be confused when they hear the word *fetch* and think they are to go get the bird.

The following chapters explain my way of teaching these skills to your dog from puppy to adult bird dog, using verbal and nonverbal commands.

Before you commit to this training, (1) go hunting with someone who has a well-trained dog, and (2) go and watch some dog trial competitions.

CHAPTER 2

STARTING YOUR PUP

Protecting
Socializing
Beginning Early Training

Many writers and trainers stress the importance of allowing a puppy to be a puppy. I agree a puppy needs to enjoy his puppyhood. However, your puppy can still be a puppy and have fun while he is learning and developing attitudes and abilities that will form the basis for his performance as a mature dog.

An important part of your dog's puppyhood is becoming his friend and letting him become your friend. Make this bond early. Part of the bonding is his jumping on you. Later, many people want to change this—but not when he's a puppy. At this time you're becoming buddies. Young puppies need this socialization. Do not yell at the little fellow or hit him. If you do, he'll soon figure that you're not his friend. If you're buddies, he'll take future training much better. If he's not sure that you're truly his friend, he may never attain his maximum potential in training. Remember, you're the only buddy he has during training. Everything (including himself) except you has the potential for causing him discomfort—birds, trash, pottering, and so forth.

Puppy-Proofing Your Home

When you have a young child in your house or when you have visiting small fry, you child-proof your house. If your pup is going to live with you in your house and/or yard, you need to puppy-proof them to make them safer places for your pup. Following are some plants and house and yard supplies that can be fatal for your pup if he ingests them.

Poisonous Vegetation

angel's trumpet	Jerusalem cherry
azalea	jimson weed
baneberry	May apple
belladonna	milkweed
bittersweet nightshade	mistletoe
buckeye	oleander
Carolina jasmine	philodendron
castor beans	poinsettia
death camas	toad stool
English holly berries	water hemlock
foxglove	

Poisonous or Dangerous House and Yard Products

antifreeze	oven cleaner
bleach	pesticides
chocolate	raisins
dangling electric cords	rat poison
dishwashing detergent	rubber balls
grapes	scrubbers: steel wool, plastic, etc.
insecticides	sponges
laundry detergent	

Socializing Your Puppy

A well-trained dog that is a pet—part of the family—as well as a hunting dog, is a joy for both children and adults. To become an enjoyable part of your family, your puppy needs to be socialized. Generally, he needs to have his chewing instincts redirected, needs to be house-trained, and needs to learn to respond appropriately to basic verbal and nonverbal commands.

The degree of socialization, like the degree of training, depends upon the purpose of your dog—what you want from him. Do you want a dog that competes in field trials? Do you want a dog that is strictly a hunting dog? Do you want a hunting dog that is also a companion? Do you want a pet that lives in the house as well as works in the field? You can have a dog that's all the above. The best hunting dogs I've had were field champions. Generally speaking, field trial dogs are the breeding base for hunting dogs.

The information in this section about socializing a pup is for those hunters or field trialers who want a bird dog that is a companion in the home as well as in the field. Dogs, like children, need to have manners if they're going to be enjoyable. *See* **Chapter 4 – Teaching Basic Commands**.

Some hunters like to have their dogs housebroken, while others are from the old school and believe a house pet can't be a good bird dog. What you want from your dog and your attitude toward dogs will determine the extent of his socialization.

Controlling Chewing

Babies need to have appropriate things to chew on when they are cutting teeth, and puppies do too. They need to have appropriate things to chew on—not your best boots—when they're teething. Opinions vary on this subject. Some people think the only thing a puppy needs to chew on is his dry puppy food. Others like to give their pup some type of chewies. Some of these items are safe; others can be dangerous. Check with your vet to find out which chewies are acceptable. I have found raw vegetables—baby carrots, broccoli, cucumber, and so forth—make excellent chewies.

Providing Toys

Some puppies enjoy playing with stuffed animals. They seem to feel the animals are their litter mates. If your dog likes these toys, let him have them, but use the same precaution you do when you give a child a stuffed animal. Be sure there are no glass eyes, etc., that could be harmful to the dog. Do not give your pup a toy you intend to use later in your training. To do so may confuse him and be counterproductive for you.

Housebreaking

To housebreak your pup, make it easy on you both. Housebreaking should be neither traumatic for the pup nor frustrating for you. Puppies do not know they're not supposed to answer the call of nature in the house. They have to be taught to relieve themselves in acceptable places. Use a crate, a leash, and supervision to accomplish this task.

Crate Training

To begin the process, buy a dog carrier (or crate) of the appropriate size, preferably the type recommended by the airlines—one in which your dog can stand comfortably and have room to curl up and sleep. The appropriate size changes as the dog grows, so unless you want to buy more than one crate, you should get one that will be the appropriate size for your dog when he is full grown. You may need to partition off part of the crate when he is small to keep him from using that part as his bathroom. Some people equip their pup's crate with a grate that allows debris to fall to the bottom of the crate, keeping the pup clean and dry.

Put the carrier in a convenient place—a place where you can get to him easily, but not where you'll be constantly stumbling over it. When your pup is in the house, keep him in the carrier all the time except when you want to play with him and can constantly supervise him.

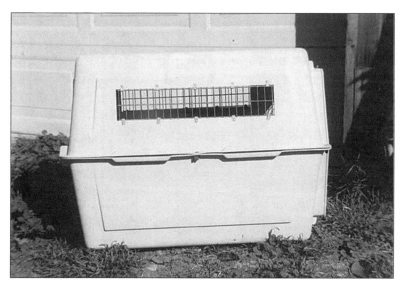

Dog crate for training and transporting

Introducing the Leash

Anytime you relocate your pup, always put him on a leash. When you do this, you're teaching him to walk on a leash, and you're making it easier for you both to take your house-training walks because you are in control. There's no need for you to chase him or yell at him. When you are through playing with him in the yard or in the house, use the leash to return him to the carrier.

Periodically, take your pup out of the crate, put him on a lead attached to his identification collar, and lead him out into the yard so he has a chance to relieve himself. Do not scold or yell at him. You are just teaching him acceptable behavior. You're happy, and your pup is happy.

Supervising Your Pup

Never let your pup out of the carrier unless you are able to constantly supervise him, and **never** take him out of the crate to play with him without first giving him the opportunity *to take care of his business* outside the house. Continue this process, and soon your puppy will understand that taking care of bodily functions is something to be done in the yard—not in the house. Soon he'll look forward to going outside.

Do not think you are being unkind or cruel to your pup by keeping him in the carrier during this training period. You are, in fact, being kind. Instinctively, dogs like to curl up in small, comfortable places—perhaps remnants of their early history of being cave dwellers.

Kenneling

While you're housebreaking your pup, start teaching him to get into and out of the carrier properly and promptly on command. *See* **Chapter 4 – Teaching Basic Commands, Kenneling**.

Beginning Yard Work

The term *yard work* is a misnomer for me. Most training referred to as *yard work* is best done in the field, rather than in the dog's home environment. In the field you can properly introduce your dog to the sound of a gun and to bird work. When you do this type of training in the field, the training is easier for you, and your dog is happier and learns more rapidly. For a more complete discussion of this training, *see* **Chapter 4 – Teaching Basic Commands, Kenneling** and **Chapter 7 – Training in the Field**.

Introducing the Art of Walking

Begin teaching your pup the art of walking on a lead as soon as you're ready to start working with him. Walking is central to my training. *See* **Chapter 4 – Teaching Basic Commands, The Art of Dog Walking**.

Introducing Retrieving

You can begin teaching your pup to retrieve at a young age. Begin the training on a table or on the ground—whichever is most convenient. If you opt for the table, put him on a low table, such as a coffee table if you're working inside the house. *See* **Chapter 5 – Teaching Retrieving**.

Value of Early Basic Training

Early basic training is a controversial issue. Some people think puppies should not receive basic training. I do. Puppies, as well as older dogs, are intelligent. If you do early training correctly—always keeping in mind that gentleness is essential—you are laying the foundation for future training. Subsequent training will be easier and more successful if the basic training has already taken place. A dog can learn ten times faster by touch or sight than he can by voice.

Enhancing Curiosity and Interest

While you are socializing your pup, introducing basic commands, and introducing yard work in the field, you also want to enhance your pup's natural curiosity and interest. Play with him—not just for the sake of playing with him as if he were just a pet—but play games (such as retrieving and holding objects) with him that develop and encourage natural instinct and curiosity.

Limiting Chasing and Pointing

Many dog owners begin enhancement training with their young pup—either in the house, yard, or both. Their objective is to get their dog interested in moving objects.

They use a fishing rod and line and tie a fluttering object such as a feather or a bird wing on the line and dangle it in front of him, getting him interested in moving objects. They flick the object around and let the pup chase it. They're showing the puppy a good time and are having fun watching him chase and point the fluttering object.

Caution: If you do this type of playing with your dog, limit it. Play someplace other than in the field where you'll be training him. Don't mis-train your dog. You don't want him to chase everything that resembles the objects you've been using to introduce pointing and chasing. Take a few pictures of the little fellow *on point* and then move on to more realistic training. If the pup gets too good at pointing what he can see, he will try to substitute this type of work for scenting. You want your dog to point a bird that he scents as well as one he sights.

Reading Your Dog's Body Language

In all phases of dog training, you must *read* your dog. Your dog can't talk, but he does have body language. This is his way of communicating with you, and you must be able to interpret what he is telling you so you can make proper responses and necessary corrections. Many trainers have problems with their dogs because they think dogs understand the full range of their vocabulary. This is not the case. Dogs understand only a few words—the ones they've been taught through repetition and stimulation.

Be attuned to your dog. Observe him and try to *read* what he is communicating to you. Each dog is different, and often the meaning of the body language depends on the breed.

Here is a list of some behaviors with generally accepted meanings:

Body Language	Meaning	Translation
Dropped tail	Confusion	What am I supposed to do? What do you want me to do?
Tail between legs	Fear	Did I do something wrong? I'm scared.
Cowering	Uneasy Frightened	I'm frightened. What's going to happen to me?
Panting or protruding tongue	Overheated or exhausted	Water me. Let me cool off and rest.
Looking over shoulder while running away	Displeasure	I'm splitting. I don't like the way you're treating me.
High tail	Pleasure or style	You make me happy. I'm being a good dog.
Lunging/over eager	Interesting, strong scent	This is a heavenly scent.
Wagging Tail (when not on birds)	Happiness	Glad to see you. I'm happy to be here.
Cocked head	Perplexed	I don't understand what you're saying.
Lying down	Confusion	You've been mean to me, or your jabbering doesn't make sense.

CHAPTER 3

COLLARS

Identifying
Protecting
Retrieving
Controlling Barking
Training
Correcting

Use collars to identify your dog, to protect him, to find him, and to train him—but not to hurt him.

Identification Collar

Always keep an identification (ID) collar on your dog.

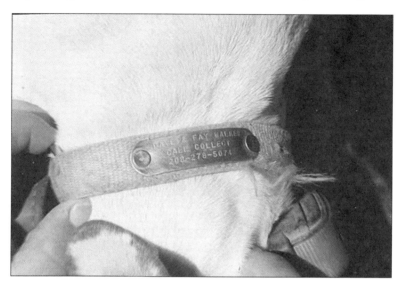

Identification Collar

Choose a sturdy collar with a center ring and a metal ID plate. The center ring will enable you to quickly and easily attach a snap, a lead, or a stake-out device because you don't have to see it to attach the tether. Choose a well-constructed collar. The metal plate must be securely attached to it.

When you get a new collar, check the brads to be sure they are of good solid construction and will not come out when you bend the collar. Carefully examine an ID collar before you buy it, or, if you're ordering it, read the description carefully.

For safety sake, you may want to use a collar with iridescent material on it. If your dog gets out at night, this collar is highly visible because the headlights of vehicles will illuminate it. It may save his life. Chain collars—not to be confused with choke collars—are a good choice for everyday use. In a multiple-dog environment, dogs will eat each other's collars—leather or nylon—which can cause serious injury or even death.

Chain collar used in multi-dog kennel

Providing Information

Put two names and two telephone numbers on the plate on the ID collar: your name and the name and number of the National Dog Registry (or the name of a company that provides the same type of service, such as Dunn's or other sporting goods suppliers).

When you register your dog with the National Dog Registry, be sure to give the dog registry at least two—preferably three—telephone numbers (yours and a friend's or someone who knows where you are at all times). This way you'll have a better chance of retrieving your dog—often from the SPCA.

Put your last name and phone number on the plate and a "Call collect" notation. Include the NDR number— 1-800-NDR-dogs (1-800-637-3647).

If your dog is lost, the person who finds him can call you or the dog registry. Do not put your dog's name on the collar. If an unscrupulous person finds your dog and decides to keep him, the name on the collar would enable that person to more easily establish a relationship with him by calling him by name.

To be on the safe side, have a micro chip implanted in the back of his neck or shoulder or have your identification number tattooed inside his thigh. Better yet, have both the micro chip and the tattoo. The tattoo is more easily identified because a wand must be waved over the dog's shoulder to ascertain if he has a micro chip implanted.

Many SPCA pounds will have a wand to scan for micro chips, but again not all do and there are several different ones. Two that are confirmed by AKC Companion Animal Enrollment are AVID and Home Again. *See* **American Kennel Club, Appendix 4 – Useful Names and Addresses**.

The tattoo and micro chip make it easier to identify your dog. Often when people find a lost dog with a tattoo on it, they will place an ad in the local paper. You may also want to put an ad in the paper offering a reward for the safe return of your dog and a note saying "No questions asked."

In addition to putting an ad in the paper, put up placards in the area. Schools are good sites. Check with UPS and FedEx drivers, postal delivery people, and the local police department.

Flair Collar

A flair collar is an iridescent collar—usually reversible, but not always—with orange on one side and yellow on the other. Put a flair collar on your dog when you're in the field; it will make him more visible and easier for you to keep track of him. These collars are available through most sporting goods places, such as Cabela's, Dunn's, or Lion Country Supply.

Note: In field trialing you may put a sleeve-type flair collar over your dog's ID collar.

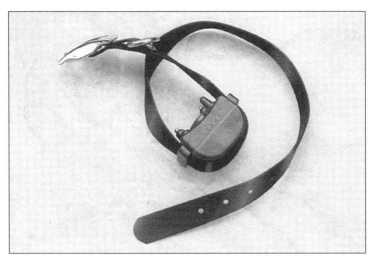

Tri-tronic® bark collar

Bark Collar

If your dog barks excessively, put a bark collar on him. A bark collar is a self-activating collar that delivers a low level of stimulation when the dog barks. Some models can be adjusted to the temperament of a particular dog. This adjustment is especially important if your dog has a sensitive nature. These collars come with simple instructions. *Tri-tronic®* makes a very dependable one. *See* **Appendix 4 – Useful Names and Addresses**.

Tracking Collar

Put a tracking collar (also called a retrieval collar) on your dog if he's a big runner who occasionally gets lost or finds chasing fur-bearing animals more exciting than hunting birds. This collar enables you to locate and retrieve your dog before he gets into serious trouble.

Many a would-be great hunting trip or field trial has come to naught because a dog has been lost, sometimes with disastrous results. Two popular tracking collars are *The Tracker®* available from Tracker and Radio Location System and the *Recovery Collar®* available from Wildlife

Materials, International. *See* **Appendix 4 – Useful Names and Addresses**.

Choke Chain

A choke chain is a type of collar which has rings at both ends. The chain drops through one of the rings and makes a collar that can be slipped over the dog's head and around his neck. By attaching a leash to one end ring, a handler can choke a dog into submission.

When should you use a choke chain? The answer is **never**. A choke chain or any other type of collar that hurts a dog has no place in my training philosophy or in my training method.

Some trainers use a choke chain for *force-breaking-to-retrieve*. As a last resort, if you feel your dog must have this type of breaking, you may want to consider taking him to a trainer who specializes in this type of training

Training Collar and Check-Cord

The training collar and the check-cord are used together and are an integral part of all phases of training. The training collar and check-cord take the feel of the stimulation out of the e-collar. I use these two devices for teaching both verbal and nonverbal commands, including reinforcing the *stand-up-and-stand-still* command.

● Teaching the *feel of the e-collar.**

● Teaching dogs to *respect birds*** when they run at them.

● Teaching the WHOA command.

● Correcting behavior problems.

feel of the e-collar—the association of the stimulation of the e-collar with that of the stimulation of the check-cord and training collar.

**respect birds—to recognize and acknowledge a trait or ability. When a dog respects a bird it means he acknowledges the bird's ability to cause him discomfort if he causes the bird to fly.*

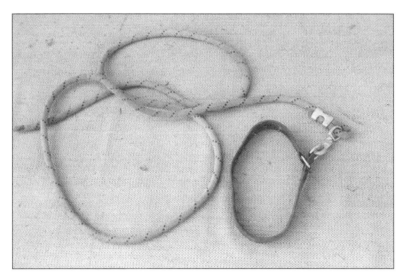

Training collar and check-cord

"No-Hurt" Training Collar

Use the *Dave Walker™ training collar.* It looks like many other collars, but it is different. It is a "no-hurt" collar. It's made of leather and does not have spikes. On the inside it has large brads with flat ends that will not injure a dog's neck.

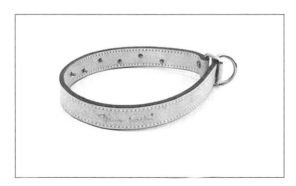

Dave Walker™ training collar

Don't get a collar that has spikes that can be filed off. Even after they're filed off, the ones I've seen are still small enough and sharp enough to injure a dog's neck. My collar is a slip-collar with a large "D" ring on one end to which the snap on the check-cord may be attached. On the other end of the collar is a slide roller that allows the collar to open and close as you use it.

Don't be misled by imitative training collars. Unless the collar has the name *Dave Walker*™ embedded in the leather, it's not my collar. Most of these copycat collars don't work in my method of training.

While there are other types of collars that can be used for training, I haven't found one I can use to teach commands—both verbal and nonverbal.

Appropriate Check-Cord

Along with the training collar, use one of my check-cords— one no longer than a 12-foot section of 9/16-inch orange-colored mountain climbing rope. This rope does not pick up stickers or other debris as it is dragged through grass, brambles, or brush. Hitchhiking debris is not only annoying; it can injure your hands.

The check-cord has a lifetime iron snap on the end attached with a solid brass clamp. The snap and the clamp give weight to the end of the cord and produce the desired sound. When you flip the check-cord, the interaction of the snap and the "D" ring produces the sound that gets the dog's attention, and he responds to whatever command you taught him.

Electronic Collar

An electronic collar (also called e-collar, electric collar, or shock collar) is a battery operated collar activated by remote control. When your dog is thoroughly familiar with the check-cord and training collar, introduce the e-collar in conjunction with them. When your dog is properly conditioned, the training collar and the e-collar become one and the same.

When you're teaching the feel of the e-collar, always do it in conjunction with another training technique and/or device that you've already introduced. In this way the dog is not feeling just the sensation of the electronic stimulation, he also feels and/or hears the other sensations he has already experienced. For example, when you start teaching your dog the nonverbal command *turn-and-go-with-me* and do not pull on the check-cord, give a little flip of the check-cord. The buckle will make a little popping sound. At the same time use the e-collar to *bump* your dog with a low level of stimulation. The sound and the feel of the stimulation become the same to him.

By introducing your dog to the e-collar in this fashion, it does what I like to think of as "taking the electricity out of the e-collar." Obviously, it doesn't remove the electricity from the collar, but it minimizes the spooking effect of the electrical stimulation because it is associated with other sensations. **Do not say anything at this time**. Using this system, your dog will accept training more readily and more rapidly and make your life and his more enjoyable as you train.

Note: The word *spook* as used in this manual is used in its informal definition meaning to frighten or to scare such as *The plop of the lures in the pool spooked the fish*. I think of using the e-collar as teaching the dog to be a good citizen. A dog is a good citizen when he follows the rules and obeys all the commands you've taught him in order to make him a well-trained, enjoyable dog.

- He stops when he's told to stop.
- He comes when he's called.
- He turns when he's supposed to turn.
- He does not pull against the check-cord.
- He gets in and out of his crate upon command.

Many people use an e-collar on their dog before he has been properly conditioned to the feel of the stimulation of it. A dog that has not been properly conditioned will often run away, run back to the handler's vehicle and cower, or just lie down and start howling. He is terrified by this new sensation.

The stimulation of the e-collar doesn't hurt dogs—it spooks them.

If you've properly conditioned your dog to the e-collar and you use it correctly and judiciously, the spooking effect of the stimulation will be mitigated.

Electronic collar and transmitter

Exercising Caution

The e-collar is a valuable tool in training dogs, but in the wrong hands—people who are uninformed or insensitive to the well-being of dogs—it can be a harmful device. All too often dogs have been ruined by careless or uninformed use of the e-collar.

The Lowest Possible Stimulation

To use the e-collar intelligently and sensitively, begin with the lowest possible stimulation in conjunction with the training collar. Timing is essential. Dogs have different levels of sensitivity. At no time do you want to make your dog jump. If he does, you've used more stimulation than you should have, or your timing is off—or both.

During the first few sessions, if you must err—do so on the side of caution. Begin with a low setting of the e-collar. Gradually move up—working several times on each level—until you reach the level appropriate for your dog. Always use the training collar in conjunction with this training.

The E-collar Alone

Never use the e-collar alone until your dog has been conditioned to the feel of it in conjunction with the training collar. Eventually, these two collars will become interchangeable in your training. Patience is the key. Some dogs take weeks to become conditioned; others take months.

Reinforcing Previous Commands

Use the e-collar to *bump* your dog to reinforce previously learned behaviors. When you're *bumping* the dog to reinforce a command he has already been taught, **DO NOT SPEAK**. If you do, your dog will associate the *bump* with you, and you don't want this to happen. If you remain silent, then your dog will blame the *bump* on something other than you—perhaps his own behavior.

Removing the E-collar

Take the e-collar off your dog when you bury him. Collars are too expensive to be buried. He should wear the e-collar all his life when he is in training or hunting. Each time you take him out of his crate or vehicle put both a training collar and an e-collar on him before his feet hit the ground until he has been conditioned to the e-collar alone.

Use the e-collar with the training collar until you are absolutely certain he's ready to be corrected with the e-collar alone.

Caution: Never leave an e-collar or a dummy e-collar on your dog when not actually training or hunting him. If you do, he'll become *collar-wise* and not respond to your commands when he's not wearing the collar. *See* **Chapter 8 – Correcting Behavior Problems, Collar Wise**.

Introducing E-collar at Right Age

People often ask me what age their dog should be when they introduce the e-collar. The answer to this question is controversial. Different people have different opinions about this subject.

You may use the e-collar on very young dogs but use it with great caution. To use the e-collar the way I do, use it to get the dog's attention—but use it in conjunction with another type of stimulation—usually the training collar and check-cord.

Another technique you might use is to gently shake your dog—using his training collar to make a noise—and immediately apply the stimulation of the e-collar. The three sensations—(1) being shaken, (2) hearing the sound of the training collar and check-cord, and (3) feeling the rubbing of the training collar—and the stimulation of the e-collar become one to him.

With a very young dog, you can get his attention by gently shaking him with your hands, shaking him with the training collar, or shaking him with the check-cord that is attached to his ID collar. All three types of shaking get his attention, but the training collar is the best. You'll make fewer mistakes using it if he is mature or large enough to wear it.

No matter what the age of the dog, whether he is four months or four years, I use everything in conjunction with the e-collar. With this method you can teach your dog to stand up when he sits or lies down and correct other similar problems.

You may use the e-collar at any age, but BE CAREFUL. **Do not move the setting up on the e-collar to increase the stimulation until you have used it several times at a lower level and you're sure your dog understands the e-collar in conjunction with the training collar or some other type of stimulation.**

Be sure you've learned to use the e-collar and check-cord and training collar simultaneously. When you use the two collars in conjunction, your dog will not feel the stimulation of the e-collar separately if you've learned to apply both of them at the same time. He perceives the stimulation to be the same as that of the training collar. He doesn't distinguish between the two.

Protecting Your Dog

Always keep the e-collar on your dog when he's outside. It's part of his working uniform. The use of this collar enables you to protect your dog from the many dangers he may encounter when he's out with you, such as not stopping when he's supposed to, running after a deer or a vehicle, or encountering a snake. The e-collar is not only a great training device; it is life insurance for your dog. It will save his life.

CHAPTER 4

TEACHING BASIC COMMANDS

Kenneling

Walking

Hee-YOH

HERE

Stop-Stand-Up-Stand-Still

Turn-and-Go-with-Me

Patterning

WHOA

Well-trained dogs are *good citizens*. People are good citizens when they respect and obey the laws of the land.

Dogs are good citizens when they respect and obey the rules taught them by their trainer.

Your dog is on his way to becoming a good citizen when he

● Gets into and out of his crate on command: responds to the verbal *KENNEL* command.

● Stops on command: responds to a nonverbal command and the verbal *WHOA* command.

● Comes to you on command: responds to a nonverbal command and verbal *HERE* command.

● *Stands-up-stands-still*: responds to a nonverbal command.

● Handles on command: responds to both verbal and nonverbal commands.

Verbal and Nonverbal Commands

To teach your dog to respond to a verbal command, choose a word you like and are comfortable with. Be consistent. Use only that word without any additional words. Some people use a whistle. The choice of a word or a whistle is a matter of preference.

When you give a verbal command, say it no louder than is necessary for your dog to hear it. You don't need to yell. He's not deaf. Dogs have excellent hearing—far better than human beings. For any verbal command, let the distance between you and your dog determine the loudness of your voice—just loud enough for him to hear you.

Verbal commands are short—usually one word or two words spoken as one—spoken words given in a quiet but clipped voice.

Nonverbal commands consist of unspoken sounds and the sense of feel. Basic commands are crucial for training your dog to be a seasoned hunter or field trial dog. The use of the e-collar as a training device—not just a correction device—is key to this training, and it takes a great deal of time and concentration to use it humanely and effectively.

At first the instructions in this chapter may seem superficial. They're not. They're simple and straightforward. Follow them carefully. Time is of the essence. Each phase of the training must be repeated over and over. You can't move on to another phase until your dog is reliable in the phase you're working on. The old adage *practice makes perfect* is truly applicable to this training.

Field Commands

Following is a brief listing of verbal and nonverbal commands. If you use these commands consistently, judiciously, and appropriately, you'll have a dog you can be proud of—hunting or field trialing.

You'll give some commands verbally (spoken). You'll give some commands nonverbally (unspoken). Sometimes you'll combine the two. For some of the commands, you may initially use a combination of the two and later drop one or the other. For example, when you're teaching the *Hee-YOH* command and your dog starts towards you; give him the verbal *HERE* command. Later, when he learns the *Hee-YOH* command means to *quarter* in front of you, you can drop the *HERE* command because he will not be coming towards you. He'll learn *HERE* as a different command. He'll have learned both at the same time.

BASIC BIRD DOG FIELD TRAINING COMMANDS

VERBAL	MEANING OF COMMAND	NONVERBAL
HEEL	Walk by my side	Flip check-cord and/or use e-collar
Hee-YOH	Come and go with me	Flip check-cord, move body and/or use e-collar in final stages
HERE	Come to me	Flip check-cord and/or use e-collar
KENNEL	Get into crate or kennel	Bump dog's rear with side of shoe while holding ID or training collar
HERE	Come out of crate or kennel	Give tug on collar
KENNEL	Jump into water, etc.	none
WHOA	Stop—right now	Stop and/or flip the check-cord and/or use the e-collar in final stages
WHUP	Keep up the good work	none
none	Don't sit down	*Bump* hock with side of shoe
none	*Stand-up-stand-still*	*Bump* hock with side of shoe, apply pressure to hindquarters
none	You may move on	Pat dog on side or other nonverbal release command
none	Look straight ahead	Straighten his head when he stops. If he moves his head, tap it with a cupped hand
none	Walk	Release by tap on side and step off

Kenneling

When you're behind your dog or alongside him, use the verbal *KENNEL* command to teach him to get into the kennel or crate. When you're in front of him and want him to come out of the kennel or crate, use the verbal *HERE* command.

You may use the *KENNEL* command to teach your dog to perform other actions, such as jumping upon a table or jumping into a body of water. It may sound a bit strange, but by using the same word the dog has to learn only one command to respond to several different situations. Just remember less is best—the fewer verbal commands, the better.

Be consistent. Use the same one-word commands. Do not use different commands or phrases, such as *get in, come out, here we go,* or *in you go.* They'll only confuse your dog.

Continue training your dog to get into and out of the carrier by putting it on a raised surface. (Later, of course, you'll put it in your transport vehicle.) First, raise the dog so he can see into the carrier. Soon, he'll get the idea that when you say *KENNEL* you want him to jump into the carrier. As your dog grows, raise the height of the carrier but keep the height of the carrier consistent with his jumping ability.

When you travel with your dog, put him in his crate. He'll feel more secure and travel better. If you put his crate in the back of your pickup truck, be sure you tie the crate down.

Encouraging a dog to get into a kennel:
Okay, okay, I'm going to jump.

When you start taking your dog to the field, you need to teach him to get in and get out of the crate or whatever conveyance you're using for transporting him. Take him by his training collar, if he has one on. If not grasp his ID collar and point his head in the direction of the crate you're putting him into. If the crate is not at his level, you may have to lift his front end up a bit to make it level with the crate.

If he jumps in, that's great. If he's reluctant, encourage him to get into the crate by *bumping* him in the rear end with the side of your foot and give the command *KENNEL*. After a few lessons, he'll jump into the kennel on command.

Some dogs will fight you to get out of the kennel. You want your dog to remain quietly in the kennel and to get out of it only on command. To teach your dog to come out of the kennel on command, when you unfasten the latch on the crate, don't open it all the way. Keep a firm hold on the door and only open it a few inches. When he tries to get out, pop the door closed. Continue popping the door— open and closed—until he learns he is not going to get out until you give him a verbal command to let him know he can leave the crate.

When he stands back and does not try to rush out, give him the verbal command *HERE* after you open the door. Continue this training until he is reliable. Some dogs respond to this command quickly. Others may be more obstinate and need several sessions before they learn the command.

Teaching the Art of Dog Walking

Fundamental to all aspects of the training is the art of walking a dog. You can use this training for any age dog. You may use it with a four-month old puppy or with a four-year old dog. It simply doesn't make any difference. The maturation of a dog's brain has more to do with training than with his chronological (calendar) age. For a more complete explanation of maturation, *see* **Chapter 1 – Choosing Your Dog, Classifying Dogs**.

If your dog is small or a young puppy, before you start training, attach the check-cord to his ID collar and let him drag it unattended for several sessions. After he is large enough to wear a training collar, put one on him and let him drag the check-cord. After your dog becomes accustomed to these training aids, begin the training process.

Walking is an integral part of teaching your dog to respond to basic commands. In conjunction with walking your dog, you will use (1) verbal commands (spoken), (2) nonverbal commands (body language), and (3) stimuli from training collar, check-cord, and e-collar to teach him basic commands.

This training is interwoven. It's not a step-by-step process. Everything is tied together. Not only does this training teach basic commands, it conditions the dog for more sophisticated future training. I think of this training as teaching dogs how to learn.

Before you begin walking and training, be sure your dog is not gun-shy. For a discussion of gun-shyness, *see* **Chapter 7 – Training in the Field, Preventing Gun-Shyness**.

Verbal *Hee-YOH* Command

The Hee-YOH command means *come-and-go-with-me-in-the-direction-I'm-facing*. At this time, teach your dog to

- walk on a slack line.

- respond to the *Hee-YOH* command (said as one word).

- learn the feel of the e-collar.

Put his full dress on him—check-cord (no longer than 12 feet), training collar, and e-collar—as soon as he is big enough to wear them. **Some dogs are more sensitive than others. Knowing your dog is crucial**. If your dog has a sensitive nature, work several sessions with him before introducing the e-collar.

Begin teaching him the feel of the e-collar (the association of the sound and feel of the check-cord, training collar in conjunction with the e-collar) as you use the *Hee-YOH* command. Begin walking. Flip the check-cord. The flip of the check-cord will produce a sound where it is fastened to the training collar and will also create a sense of feeling from the training collar. At the same time give the verbal command *Hee-YOH* to teach him *turn-and-go-with-me*.

The flip of the check-cord gets your dog's attention by the sound and the motion. To produce the desired effect, use a training collar that is flexible. If the part of the training collar that runs from the dog's neck to the snap and ring at the end of the check-cord is not flexible, you'll be unable to produce the sound you want to get your dog's attention—the sound that is necessary when used in conjunction with the e-collar. Flip the check-cord and simultaneously deliver the stimulation to the e-collar, and your dog associates the two stimuli. By teaching him the feel of the e-collar at this time, you'll find teaching subsequent commands much easier.

Keep the check-cord loose by turning your dog with the *Hee-YOH* command. Your dog—as all dogs tend to do—will pull against a taut line. You can control your dog more easily if you don't have a taut line. A slack line is easier on both you and your dog. The two of you will enjoy the training more, and neither of you will be as tired at the end of the lesson if you've not been pulling on each other. A slack line will also let you give the correct flips of the check-cord to produce nonverbal commands.

Let your dog get out about 3 or 4 feet in front of you (or closer at first). Once there, more than likely he'll pull on the lead. Give a little flip of the check-cord (a nonverbal command) and at the same time give your dog the verbal *Hee-YOH* command to let him know you want him to stop pulling on the lead and turn and go with you. When he turns, the check-cord automatically becomes slack, signaling to him he's responding correctly. Repeatedly say the command *Hee-YOH*. You want him to learn the word. At this time you want to teach him to walk on a loose lead and to turn and go with you. More often than not, your dog will be happy to go with you because he wants to be near you. Some headstrong dogs will be reluctant to go with you. If your dog refuses to go with you after a few tries, be more firm with the check-cord and training collar.

Verbal *HERE* Command

At the same time you're teaching your dog to turn and go with you (basic patterning), teach him to come to you. For this training, use the word *here* because it is sharper than the word *come* and travels farther with less volume. Just as you do when teaching your dog to *turn-and-go-with-you,* give the check-cord a little flip, stop, and give him the verbal command *HERE*.

Stop walking and give the verbal *HERE* command only after he has come to you on his own during the walking, turning, and responding to the *Hee-YOH* command sessions. He may come to you just because he likes you and wants to be near you. If he does come to you, pet him. Begin by stroking him, starting at his head and working toward his hindquarters, using only your fingertips at this time. As you near his hindquarters, begin using more of your fingers and the palm of your hand, gradually applying pressure to his hips. Do not wear gloves when you're petting your dog. He likes the feel of your hand. Don't talk to him during this training session. At this time, use only the command *HERE*.

Use the e-collar in conjunction with the training collar and check-cord to reinforce the *HERE* command. Let your dog get out about 3 or 4 feet. Then, just as you did when you introduced the *Hee-YOH* command, flip the check-cord and say *HERE*—softly, not loudly or harshly—and simultaneously *bump* your dog with the e-collar. Be sure to perform these acts at exactly the same time. You are continuing to teach your dog the feel of the e-collar and training him to associate the *bump* with the verbal command *HERE*.

Nonverbal *STOP* Command

Teach your dog the nonverbal *stop* command only after he has come to you on his own while you're teaching him to walk on a loose lead, to respond to the *Hee-YOH* command, and to learn the feel of the e-collar.

Keep him in full dress (check-cord, training collar, and e-collar). Take a few steps with your dog on a loose lead. Stop, and at the same time you stop, give a flip of the check-cord. If your dog doesn't stop, resume walking. When you stop the next time, simultaneously flip the check-cord and deliver a low level of stimulation to the e-collar.

Continue walking him, stopping, and flipping the check-cord. Sometimes *bump* him with the e-collar but not every time. Do not use the e-collar more than twice in the first lesson. Use the check-cord by itself, but don't use the e-collar by itself at this time.

Do not add a verbal command at this time. Reward your dog for stopping by stroking him gently from his head to his hindquarters, using only the tips of your fingers, putting a little pressure on his hindquarters. He'll resist the pressure and will stand taller. This is the beginning of teaching him to *stand-up-stand-still*.

Your dog has learned the nonverbal stop command when he consistently stops when you

- stop and flip the check-cord.

- combine the flip of the check-cord and the e-collar.

- stop without flipping the check-cord.

Your goal is for him to stop when you stop without your doing anything. Continue training until he consistently stops when you do. Stopping on a nonverbal command is a necessary part of later training.

Stop-Stand-Up-Stand-Still Command

The nonverbal *stop-stand-up-stand-still* stance is important. It shows good manners; it shows your dog is obedient; and it makes him look better when you're hunting, field trialing, or showing him. More importantly, however, it shows he will take training. This stance is the basis for future training.

This training can be used for both *soft* dogs and *tough* dogs. Soft dogs are sensitive and respond to gentle training methods. This in no way means these dogs are not good bird dogs. It simply means that because of their temperament, they do not respond to harsh training methods. A tough dog is usually headstrong and is generally thought of as being a dog that will respond only to heavy-handed training. My method works with so-called tough dogs because they, too, like to be praised. Both types are eager to please because they like the praise—petting. They want to do what you want them to do, and their desire to please is derived from pleasure—not pain.

To teach the nonverbal command *stop-stand-up-stand-still*, begin by walking your dog. Let him get out about a foot or so in front of you, flip the check-cord and training collar and stop. Your dog already knows this nonverbal command and will stop. Then start walking by your dog—very slowly—with a slack check-cord in your hand. As you walk past your dog, in all probability he will begin to move with you. At this time stop, flip the check-cord and at the same time *bump* him with the e-collar, keeping the stimulation at a low level.

Straightening Your Dog's Head

When your dog stops, he'll probably turn his head to look at you because he wants to know what you're doing. You want his head to be straight—looking forward—not twisted around looking at you. At this time grasp his muzzle with your left hand—gently but firmly. At the same time, give a slight shaking motion to the check-cord and training collar. Transfer the check-cord to your left hand, and with your right hand gently stroke him from his ears back—applying a little pressure just as you did when you first started stroking.

Straightening a dog's head: Correction 1

If he still moves his head after you stop him, grasp his muzzle with your left hand and use the check-cord and training collar to shake him. Continue walking him and repeat the procedure until you can get out in front of him 2 or 3 feet.

Each session should take no more than a few minutes, and the entire session should not exceed 15 or 20 minutes when you start. After a few sessions, you may become more demanding. When he turns to look at you, again grasp his muzzle and straighten up his head so he's facing forward. Cup your right hand slightly and gently clap it under his right ear, making a little smacking sound.

Straightening a dog's head: Correction 2

Correcting a Dog that Sits Down

When you're teaching your dog to *stand-up-stand-still*, you'll be walking him. When you stop, more than likely your dog will stop also. If he doesn't stop, give him a little flip of the check-cord and training collar so that he will stop.

When he does stop, he'll probably sit down—most dogs do—especially, if you haven't done a thorough job in the *stand-up-stand-still* work. If he tries to sit down, don't pick him up. You want to teach him to stand up, and if you pick him up, you'll defeat your purpose. Anticipating his sitting down, be ready for him. Slip your foot under him when he stops and tries to sit down. Gently bump his hocks backward with your shoe. Never bump his hocks upward because you'll hit him in the belly. You could injure him. At the same time, press down on his hindquarters. Use the side of your shoe to *bump* him. Don't use the toe or the sole of your shoe because they could hurt him. If you're working him on your left side, *bump* him on his left hock.

If you're working him on your right side, *bump* him on his right hock.

Put your right hand on his hips and apply gentle but firm pressure. If he moves, gently jiggle his head, which you are holding in your left hand. This gentle shaking will make him aware of his head instead of what he wants to do with his rear end. When you apply pressure to his hindquarters, his natural instinct is to push back (which he will do), and pushing back makes him stand up.

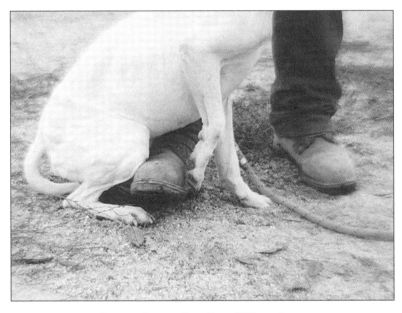

Correcting a dog for sitting down

Sometimes he'll sit down even with your foot under him. Don't be discouraged. Use the same procedure. Move the foot he's sitting on, gently *bump* his hocks backward, straighten his head, and apply pressure to his hindquarters. Continue this procedure until he learns that when you stop, he must *stop-stand-up-stand-still.*

If your dog is too small to wear a training collar, attach the check-cord to his ID collar. You can bring him back with it instead of chasing him or scolding him. When you're working with an extremely young pup—4 to 6 months old—remember gentleness is absolutely essential.

If possible, teach the *stop-stand-up-stand-still* command in the field between birds as you do bird work. *See* **Chapter 7 – Training in the Field**. If you don't have access to a place where you can teach this command while you're working birds, find a place—other than his home environment—where you can begin this phase of training. Continue walking your dog, teaching him to *stop-stand-up-stand-still* and letting you get out in front of him as you pretend to flush birds. At this time you're only pretending to flush birds, but, eventually, as you progress with your training, you'll actually be flushing.

Do not use verbal commands at this time.

In fact, say nothing to him at all because it will confuse him. In my training videos, I stress the importance of nonverbal commands—which I use in all my training—by showing a trainer with a piece of duct tape over his mouth. Do not be misled (as some people who use these videos have been) and misinterpret this image, thinking that these commands are silent. They're not silent because a rattling sound is emitted from the connection of the buckle and the snap on the check-cord when the check-cord is given a little flip. The dog responds to the noise.

Patterning

Teach your dog to pattern (also called *quarter*) at the same time you teach him to walk, turn, and go with you. The procedures are interrelated. Turning and going with you is a close-range situation. The hunting pattern is simply an extension or long-range version of this close-range patterning. At first when you turn your body, make a 90-degree turn. Later, as your dog develops, you can make a 180-degree turn.

On Foot

At this time, you want to teach your dog to walk on a slack line and turn and go with you in response to both verbal and nonverbal commands. Give him a nonverbal command—turning your body—to let him know he is supposed to *turn-and-go-with-you.* Choose and use a one-word verbal command to teach your dog to walk on a loose lead, and at the same time teach him to turn and go with you in the direction you're facing. (I use the command *Hee-YOH.*)

Dog being trained to quarter

On Horseback

Before you begin teaching your dog to pattern while you're on a horse, be sure he knows all the commands you taught him when you were working him on foot. Some dogs need very little training—one or two lessons—on foot before being trained on horseback.

Remove the training collar and attach the check-cord to his ID collar. You'll be working him with the e-collar and check-cord. Having the check-cord on him when he's running in front of the horse will help him with getting the feel of the e-collar. Some dogs will do better horseback patterning if you do some patterning on foot using the check-cord, training collar, and e-collar right before you start the horseback patterning.

If your dog is having trouble learning, attach the check-cord to his ID collar, still keep the e-collar on him, and let him drag the check-cord as he is running. This procedure seems to have a calming effect on a dog. He becomes more responsible and easier to handle. When he drags the check-cord, he feels secure. He seems to remember his early training first with the training collar and check-cord and later the addition of the e-collar.

Use the verbal command *Hee-YOH* (or whatever command you've chosen) and turn your horse the same way you turned your body when you were working him on foot. If your dog doesn't respond by turning and going in the direction you're riding, deliver a low level of stimulation to the e-collar to get him to turn at the same time you give the verbal command. If he is a very young pup that you haven't trained with the e-collar, call him to you and start him over in the direction you're going. Do this training at close range until he responds appropriately. Then you can let him range out farther and farther. He learned the nonverbal command first—the flip of the check-cord—and it was reinforced with the verbal command *Hee-YOH*, so he knows when he hears the verbal command he is to turn and go with you. In this way you can direct your dog's pattern at a great distance. All he has to do is hear your verbal command.

WHOA Command

You've already taught your dog verbal and nonverbal *HERE* commands and reinforced them with the stimulation of the e-collar. He unfailingly comes to you on command. You've already taught him the nonverbal *stop-stand-up-stand-still* command and reinforced it with the stimulation of the e-collar, and he unfailingly *stops-stands-up-stands-still* on command. Now, you're ready to introduce the verbal *WHOA* command.

Note: The nonverbal *stop-stand up-stand-still* command means the same thing as the verbal *WHOA* command.

Let your dog get out a few feet in front of you—about 3 or 4 feet, just as you did when you were teaching him the nonverbal *stop-stand-up-stand-still* command. After he learns what the word *whoa* means, you may use it at any range. Simultaneously, with the nonverbal command, say the word *whoa*, give the check-cord a little flip, and ease out in front of him. Be ready with the e-collar just in case he doesn't stop or moves after he has stopped. Dogs tend to move after they've stopped when they hear a new command and don't know what to make of it.

When your dog hears the command *WHOA*, he, most likely, will tilt his head to one side because this is the first word you've spoken to him during this training session. Say the word *whoa* over and over each time your dog moves. He will probably move until he learns the word *whoa* means he is not supposed to move. Your dog will stop because you've previously taught him to stop when you give a flip to the check-cord. Now, you slowly ease out in front of him with one hand on the e-collar button (check-cord in the other) ready to *bump* him if he tries to follow you. Frequently he will.

Move less than a foot at a time and not more than two feet in front of him. While you're standing in front of him, take his muzzle in your hand and pet him for letting you move out in front of him without his moving. Never *bump* your dog with the e-collar after you've passed his head while you're moving out in front of him. If you do, he'll start dropping in the front as he sees you and will associate the feel of the e-collar with you, and you don't want this to happen. Return to his side. Be ready with your hand on the e-collar and the check-cord in your other. If he moves, flip the check-cord and bump him with the e-collar. If he doesn't move, give him a tap on the side to let him know its okay to move to a new location.

Note: Again, it is the sound that is produced at the end of the check-cord that is attached to the training collar that gets his attention, and the stimulation of the e-collar reinforces previous knowledge.

After he has obeyed all the commands and stood still when you come back to pet him, don't do any more training in this location. You've given him both a verbal and nonverbal *WHOA* commands, moved out in front of him, and have come back and petted him. End the session on this happy note, put him in his crate, and again pet him for doing well.

Important: From now on, the use of the combination of the check-cord and the training collar is interchangeable with the stimulation of the e-collar. Your dog will respond to either type of stimulation—the *bump* of the e-collar or the popping sound of the training collar. These three commands—*HERE, stop-stand-up-stand-still*, and *WHOA*— are pivotal to sophisticated bird work, which is your ultimate goal.

Limiting Verbal *WHOA* Command

The *WHOA* command is not as important as other commands. It's overused and abused by far too many dog trainers and owners. It's not a magical word, and it isn't a word to be used in most training. It has a specific purpose. It is not an all-purpose word that can be bandied around without causing problems. Never use the word *whoa* when your dog is on point, before he establishes point, when he is honoring, when you're teaching him to honor, or to replace another command that has a specific purpose.

Anytime you use a verbal command when your dog is involved in his work, he'll move or start flagging, especially when he is trying to point, is on point, or is honoring. If he could talk, he'd probably tell you he's confused. He thinks he is doing what you have taught him. When you talk to him and use a verbal command he doesn't understand, he still tries to come up with a response.

Teaching Your Dog to Heel

Teaching your dog to walk on a loose lead is not the same as teaching him to *HEEL*. Teach the social command *HEEL* only after you've completed the fieldwork. After your dog has learned to consistently respond to the following basic field commands—all taught with the *Hee-YOH* command—and has been conditioned to the e-collar, you're now ready to teach him to *HEEL*:

Hee-YOH: Turn and go with me.

HERE: Come to me right now.

Stand-up-stand-still: Stand up tall and be still.

WHOA: Stop right now.

If you've already taught your dog to walk on a slack line, you'll find teaching him to *HEEL* will be easy. As you teach your dog to heel, repeat the command *HEEL* over and over—just as you would if you were teaching a child a new word. When you're teaching a child a new word such as *fork*, you probably hold it up for the child to see it. You have no object to hold up for your dog, but have patience. If you say the word often enough, he'll eventually learn what you want him to do when you say that word. Remember, a dog can learn ten times faster by touch or sight than he can by voice.

A dog is heeling properly when he responds to the verbal command *HEEL* given only once—when you begin to walk with him—and his head is even with your legs and he stops in position when you stop. He's not heeling properly if you've had to give the verbal command more than once, if he gets ahead of you, or if he pulls on the lead.

To teach your dog to *HEEL*, put him in full dress (training collar, check-cord, and e-collar). Face the direction you intend to walk and take your check-cord in your right hand behind you so you can give a little jerk when you want to make a correction. Bring your dog to your left side with his head pointing straight to the front. Give him a little tap on the side to release him. Give the check-cord a flip to create a sound where it is attached to the buckle of the training collar. Give the verbal command *HEEL* in a clear, crisp tone. He knows the word because you've said it over and over.

Begin walking, stepping out on your left foot. Since most people are right handed, the *heel* position is usually carried out on the left side. If you're left handed and don't intend to enter your dog in shows, you may want to train him to *HEEL* on your right side. If this is the case, place him on your right side and step off with your right foot. Otherwise, step off with your left.

At first use the check-cord, training collar, and e-collar together. If he doesn't stop when you do or pulls on the lead, *bump* him with the e-collar—using the lowest level of stimulation that he is used to—at the same time that you give the verbal command *HEEL* and flip the check-cord. Periodically, stop and make him stop when you do. Praise him when he *heels* correctly.

Continue this training, using the check-cord, training collar, and e-collar until your dog consistently responds to the simultaneous commands. This shows he is ready for the e-collar without the training collar.

Leave the training collar and check-cord on him, but don't flip the check-cord. Just use the verbal command *HEEL* and the stimulation of the e-collar. When he consistently responds to the command and the stimulation of the e-collar, remove the check-cord and training collar and finish the training by using only a low level of stimulation to reinforce the verbal command *HEEL*. Now you're on your way. You can control him when he isn't wearing the training collar and check-cord.

A Resistant Dog

If your dog is resistant to the training and continues to pull on the check-cord, deliver a low level of stimulation with the e-collar at the same time you flip the check-cord and tell him to *HEEL*. Continue this training until he is reliable.

Your Hunting Dog

Some hunters want their dog to *heel*, and others don't think it's important or necessary. If your dog is a family pet in addition to being your hunting partner, you may want to teach him to *heel*. When you take him for a walk, he should be being taken for a walk—not taking you for a walk by pulling you down the street.

The training is the same for teaching any dog to *heel*. Instead of working your dog on the left side as is customary, you should work him on your right side if you shoot left-handed. In this way you can carry your gun in your left hand and not interfere with the control of your dog.

Training for Competition

If you're training your dog for competition, get the complete set of rules for the events in which he'll be competing and train him to meet the requirements.

All the training in this book is applicable to both field trial and hunting dogs. You just have to learn the competition rules operative in field trialing. Any skills or abilities required in competition are covered thoroughly in this manual. This book is a bird dog training book. It's not a manual for horseback riding; however, horseback riding is a necessary skill for any serious field trialer.

CHAPTER 5

TEACHING RETRIEVING

HOLD

GIVE

DEAD

Walking

Reaching

Holding

Releasing

Introducing Retrieving

Young dogs, including young puppies, can be trained to be reliable retrievers. You may begin training in the house on a coffee table, outside on a picnic bench, on the tailgate of your truck, or on the ground. It is a simple but powerful training technique that can be used with the most sensitive dogs, and it is just as effective as the more rigorous force training.

Some dogs have an innate inclination to retrieve and learn rapidly. Other dogs are reluctant to retrieve and require more time and more vigorous training. Whether your dog is naturally inclined to retrieve or is reluctant, training him to retrieve when he is young is much easier than when he is older. If you begin teaching your dog to retrieve at a young age, it doesn't matter whether he's a reluctant retriever or an eager retriever; he can be trained to be a reliable retriever.

There are two types of training used in teaching dogs to retrieve. The temperament of your dog will determine which type of training you do. (1) Dogs that are naturally inclined to retrieve can be trained by praising them— petting. (2) Dogs that are reluctant to retrieve need to be trained by both discipline and praise. This method is commonly called *force breaking*.

No matter which type you do, the sooner you have your dog walking with a dummy or bird in his mouth the easier the training will be for you both.

To teach a dog to retrieve by either method, you have to teach him to open his mouth, hold a training dummy (or a bird if you're training in the field), and respond to the commands *HOLD* and *GIVE*. Most dogs easily and quickly respond to these commands because they enjoy this training because they get lots of petting and associate the petting with the commands.

Later, you'll need to teach your dog to respond to the command *DEAD* or *HUNT DEAD*. This command is usually easy because your dog can see the bird fall.

Basic Retrieval Commands

Verbal	Meaning	Nonverbal
FETCH	Open your mouth	Apply pressure
HOLD	Keep object in your mouth	Bump or cuff
GIVE	Drop the object in my hand	Hold out hand and/or apply pressure to body part
FETCH	Reach for the object	
FETCH	Go get the object and return it to me	
DEAD or HUNT DEAD	Find a dead bird	

HOLD Command

Put your dog on a table or some surface comfortable for both you and your dog to work on. Put a lead on him and begin the training session.

Teach your dog to hold an object in his mouth by placing it in his mouth. The object should be appropriate to the size of the dog. A small paint roller works well as a mini retrieving dummy for a very young or small puppy. A retrieving dummy—sized to fit a particular dog—works for larger dogs. You may purchase retrieving dummies from dog training supply houses, such as Dunn's or Cabela's.

To get him to open his mouth, put your hand over his muzzle and squeeze his lips against his teeth. When he opens his mouth, place the roller or dummy in it and give the verbal command *HOLD*, and at the same time *bump* him gently but firmly with the back of your hand under his chin with your other hand. Stroke him gently around the ears and top of his head while he is holding the dummy. Keep *bumping* him under the chin until he stops trying to spit it out.

During this process keep repeating the word *hold* over and over until he understands what it means. Never hold the dummy in his mouth. If you do, he'll expect you to do it for him.

Some dogs require more firmness than others. Continue stroking and bumping him under the chin if you need to help him. After a time he'll realize that you're not going to hurt him, will respond to the stroking, and will hold the dummy in his mouth when you start walking with him. The sooner you can walk with him while he is holding the dummy without your assistance, the more rapidly the training will progress.

Caution: Do not add any words to the commands, such as *good boy, hold it for me*, or *that's great.* If you do, your training will not be as successful as it could be.

Dog being bumped under chin while holding a dummy

GIVE Command

When your dog stops resisting and holds the dummy, continue petting him for a short time. Then say *GIVE*. If he doesn't open his mouth to *GIVE*, roll the dummy a bit, and usually he'll spit it out in your hand. Immediately, repeat the process. Put the dummy back in his mouth and give the verbal command *HOLD*. Let him hold it for a few seconds and then tell him to *GIVE*. Do this procedure three or four times in this session.

As you continue training, have him hold the dummy for progressively longer periods of time. Throughout this training keep repeating the command *GIVE* over and over until he learns what the word give means. Always put the dummy back in his mouth and give the verbal command *HOLD*. Immediacy is crucial. The quicker you get the dummy back into his mouth the faster he will learn.

Walking and Holding a Dummy

After your dog is reliable with the *HOLD* and *GIVE* commands, it's time to move to the next phase of the training—walking with the dummy in his mouth.

You may work on the table with him, or you may put him on the ground. Repeat the previous procedures—reviewing *HOLD* and *GIVE*. All you want him to do at this time is to just take a few steps with the dummy in his mouth. Before you put the dummy in his mouth, walk with him and pet him. He'll enjoy the walking and the petting and will be less resistant to walking with the dummy.

Put the dummy in his mouth and say *HOLD*. While he is holding the dummy in his mouth, walk alongside him and pet him. Then move with him, keeping the dummy in his mouth by bumping him under the chin if need be. Encourage him to take a few steps by tugging on his lead and giving him the verbal command *HERE* as you move with him.

Dog walking and holding a dummy in his mouth

As soon as he's comfortable moving with the dummy in his mouth, put him in full dress—training collar, check-cord, and e-collar. If he is small or very young or both, just use a check-cord attached to his ID collar and an e-collar because a training collar would be too heavy for a little dog.

Gradually increase the distance your dog is traveling with the dummy in his mouth. If he tries to spit it out or drops it, instead of *bumping* him under the chin, grasp him by his ID collar and shake him. At the same time, deliver a low level of stimulation and put the dummy back into his mouth.

If your dog is large enough to wear a training collar, when you make the correction, flip the check-cord to cause the buckle to make a sound at the same time you deliver the stimulation of the e-collar.

Continue this process using the ID or training collar until he is comfortable with the procedures and responds appropriately to commands. For a more complete discussion of using the e-collar, *see* **Chapter 3 – Collars, Electronic Collar**.

Retrieving a Feathered Dummy

After your dog demonstrates he can consistently *HOLD*, *GIVE*, and walk with a dummy in his mouth, exchange the dummy for an object covered with bird wings. Be sure the object is appropriate for the size of your dog. You may use a block of wood, a soup can, or a stick. Use the feathered dummy and play with him to get him interested in it. Follow the same procedures you used in training him to walk with the other dummy.

Dog holding a feathered dummy in his mouth

When he is comfortable walking with the feathered dummy, start training him to retrieve it. While holding the check-cord, toss the dummy out 3 or 4 feet. He may run to the dummy, pick it up, and bring it back to you. This is an ideal situation, so you pet him for a job well done and continue this training.

If he doesn't go to the dummy, you need to teach him what you want him to do. Take him to the dummy, put it in his mouth, give him the command *HOLD*, and walk with him back to where you were standing. Hold out your hand and tell him to *GIVE*. When he gives you the dummy, pet him for a job well done. If he tries to spit the dummy out or drops it, simultaneously shake him and deliver a low level of stimulation. Put the dummy back into his mouth and say *HOLD*. Continue this process until he's reliable.

He may go to the dummy and not pick it up. If he does, go to him and put it in his mouth and tell him to *HOLD*. Then walk him back to where you were standing. Hold out your hand and tell him to *GIVE*. When he gives you the dummy, pet him. Again, you may have to help him hold it in his mouth by bumping him under the chin. Never try to help him by holding it in his mouth.

He may go to the dummy and pick it up but not bring it back to you. If this is what he does, give him the verbal command *HERE*, and tug on his lead to get him to come to you. When he comes to you, hold out your hand and tell him to *GIVE*. Pet him for doing a good job.

Retrieving Dead Birds

Caution: Be sure you condition your dog to the gun before beginning this training. Don't shoot over him if you've not trained him to the gun. If this is the case, treat him as if he were a gun-shy dog. Follow the procedures in **Chapter 7 – Training in the Field, Preventing Gun-Shyness** and get him conditioned to the gun before you shoot over him.

After he has successfully retrieved and delivered a feathered dummy on command, exchange the feathered dummy for a freshly killed bird. Work with him until he's comfortable holding it, walking, and giving it to you on command. When you begin working with freshly killed birds, always fire over your dog.

Still holding the check-cord, take a freshly killed bird, toss it out 6 or 8 feet and see if he'll retrieve it. If he picks the bird up but doesn't bring it back to you, give the verbal command *HERE* and tug on the check-cord. *See* **Chapter 4 – Teaching Basic Commands, Verbal *HERE* Command**.

If he drops the bird at any time, make the correction with the check-cord and stimulation of the e-collar. Depending upon how resistant your dog is to the training, you may have to increase the level of stimulation. Use the same training techniques you used when you were working him with the feathered dummy.

Note: You must have used the e-collar to teach your dog to hold the bird before you increase the stimulation.

When your dog brings the bird back to you consistently, he's ready for the next step in training: retrieving birds in the field. Follow the procedures in the following section: **Dogs that Like to Retrieve, Retrieving Birds in the Field**.

Dogs That Like to Retrieve

Dogs that enjoy retrieving and seem to do it naturally can easily be turned into reliable retrievers by shooting birds for them. Dogs are never reliable in competition until they hold the bird and release it only upon command. If your dog shows a natural tendency to retrieve, begin the early retrieving training as discussed above.

Retrieving Birds in the Field

Continue training when you're working your dog in the field. Shoot a bird for him, go to the bird with him, hold the check-cord in your hand, but give him the full length of it. By doing this, you are giving him the opportunity to pick up the bird and come back to you.

When he picks up the bird, more than likely he'll bring it back to you. If he doesn't, give him a soft verbal command *HERE* and tug on the check-cord to get him to come back to you. When he comes back to you with the bird, hold out your hand and say *GIVE*. He may put it in your hand, or he may drop it at your feet. Most dogs will drop the bird at your feet or drop it before they get to you.

Releasing Birds on Command

After your dog becomes reliable—goes to the bird, picks it up and brings it to you, but drops it instead of holding it— it is now time to teach him to hold the bird until you give him the verbal command *GIVE*. Put the bird in his mouth and say *HOLD*. If he drops the bird, correct him using the check-cord and training collar.

Caution: Never use the e-collar on your dog when he has a bird in his mouth until he has been taught the *HOLD* command with the e-collar.

Continue this training in the field. Kill a bird for him and toss it out several times, firing your gun, and commanding him to *HOLD* the bird until you tell him to *GIVE*. Put that bird away, shoot another one for him, and continue the training. Now you have a happy dog. End the session on this positive note and put your dog in his crate or kennel.

During your next training session, repeat the same procedures, but shoot two or more birds for him or throw a dead bird several times. Fire your gun each time you toss the bird. Keep him in full dress at all times. If he drops the bird, make the correction immediately. Sometimes it takes a long time to teach a dog to hold the bird after he has brought it to you.

With him still on the check-cord, keep working him on birds until he consistently brings them to you and holds them until you tell him to *GIVE*. When you feel he is totally reliable, drop the check-cord and see if he'll bring the bird back to you on his own and hold it until you tell him to *GIVE*. If he errs, make the correction immediately with the e-collar so he will know that what he did is what caused the discomfort.

Caution: Never start a dog off on retrieving by letting him go to the bird alone. If you do, you may create problems such as the dog grabbing the bird, running away with it, burying it, or eating it.

Force Breaking Mature Dogs

In all retrieving, your dog must demonstrate he can hold and carry a freshly killed bird in his mouth before you advance him. Some dogs are easier to train to retrieve than others, but all dogs can be taught to retrieve using whatever method works for each particular dog. One method is commonly called *force breaking. Force breaking* is a term used to identify the type of training used to teach a dog to do something he is not naturally inclined to do or something he just doesn't like to do.

If you condition your dog properly to the commands and responses when you begin this training, the rest of it will be easy for you both. The key to this training is to take more time and use less force. Rome was not built in a day, and teaching your dog to retrieve will not be done in one day. If you take more time and less force when you begin this training, you'll be using less force when you're finishing the training. Praise your dog by petting him when he makes a correct response. In this way you're telling him he's doing the right thing and you're pleased with him. All these procedures take time. **Don't rush your dog.**

Teaching *FETCH, HOLD,* and *GIVE*

You can do this training on the ground, but it can get pretty uncomfortable—makes your back hurt. For the sake of your comfort, you might want to begin this type of training on a table with a short chain in the middle and attach your dog to it by snapping his ID collar to it. A wooden cable spool about 7 feet wide makes a good training table. Put a training collar with a check-cord attached and an e-collar on your dog in front of his ID collar.

Round training table

Getting Your Dog's Mouth Open

The first thing you need to do when you begin force breaking your dog to retrieve is to get him to open his mouth so you can insert an object in it—a dummy, a bird, or whatever you're using to teach him *FETCH*. There are several ways to get a dog to open his mouth. The most common way (as discussed above) is to apply pressure to his teeth. If that doesn't work, apply pressure to some other part of his body. Some people apply pressure to the ear, and others apply pressure to the toe.

Some dogs may be more sensitive to ear pressure, and other dogs may be more sensitive to toe pressure. Use the verbal command *FETCH*. Repeat it over and over until your dog understands the meaning of the word.

Applying Pressure to Teeth

To get your dog to open his mouth, put your hand over his muzzle and squeeze his lips against his teeth. Give the verbal command *FETCH*. Usually, it takes little pressure to get a dog to open his mouth.

Force breaking: applying pressure to teeth

Applying Pressure to Ear

To apply pressure to your dog's ear, take a round-headed key with no sharp edges and use your index finger to place the round part of the key inside his ear—two-thirds of the way into his ear. Place your thumb on the outside of the ear. Using your thumb and index finger squeeze the key against his ear and give the command *FETCH*. Keep saying *FETCH* and applying as much pressure as needed until he opens his mouth. For most dogs it doesn't take much pressure.

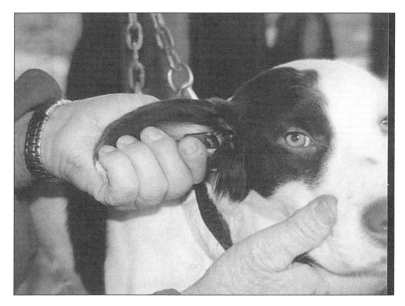

Force breaking: applying pressure to ear

As soon as your dog opens his mouth, insert the dummy and tell him to *HOLD*. Release the pressure on his ear at the same time. Timing is crucial. Pet him while he is holding the dummy. If he tries to spit it out or drops it, *bump* him under his chin until he holds it. If he drops or spits out the dummy, apply more pressure to his ear, saying *FETCH* as you put it back into his mouth.

After he quits rejecting it, give him the command *GIVE* and take hold of the dummy. He may just spit it out. If so pet him. If he doesn't spit it out, roll the dummy a bit and say *GIVE*. He'll probably be happy to spit it out. Continue this training until he is reliable on opening his mouth, holding the dummy, and releasing it on command. Remember to keep repeating all the verbal commands. He needs to learn all these words in his first few lessons.

Getting a dog to hold a large dummy

Applying Pressure to Toe

This training may be done on a table or on the ground, whichever you find works best for you. If you do the work on the ground, you don't have to worry about getting a table, and you don't have to go from the table to the ground training and back to the table if your dog has a problem. Just drive a stake in the ground, put his training collar, check-cord, and e-collar on him and begin training.

Force breaking: applying pressure to toe

Use a small nylon cord about 3 feet long and a bit smaller in diameter than a standard pencil—clothesline works fine. Tie a knot in each end of the cord. Put a clove hitch on your dog's leg about 8 or 10 inches above his toes and put a half-hitch around his inside toe, snubbing it up tautly.

Pull the cord while applying pressure and give the command *FETCH*. Keep repeating the word *FETCH*, and, eventually, he'll learn what it means. This is a new experience, and it scares him. Repeat the command until he opens his mouth. As soon as he opens his mouth, put the dummy in it and release the pressure immediately. Timing is crucial. Give him the command *HOLD* and begin petting him.

After you've finished petting him, take hold of the dummy and say *GIVE*. As with all verbal commands, say the word over and over until he learns its meaning. More than likely he'll be happy to spit it out. If he doesn't, take one end and roll it a bit, and he should spit it out.

Continue this procedure, holding the cord in your hand. If he tries to spit the dummy out or drops it at any time, use the cord to apply pressure to his toe and simultaneously flip the check-cord and bump him with stimulation of the e-collar. Keep training your dog until he is reliable: He consistently responds to the commands without pressure.

Walking and Carrying a Dummy

Now start walking him while he is holding the dummy—one or two steps at a time. As you start walking, say *HERE* and give a little tug on his check-cord. When you first start this training, you'll be walking alongside your dog. Continue using the *HERE* command and tugging on the check-cord (if necessary) and increase the distance he walks, still holding the dummy in his mouth.

If he drops the dummy or tries to spit it out, apply pressure to his ear or toe and simultaneously bump him with stimulation of the e-collar. Put the dummy back into his mouth and tell him to *HOLD*.

When he holds the dummy, release the pressure at once. Continue training until he consistently walks while carrying the dummy and going with you on command.

Reaching for Dummy

In the next phase of the training, teach your dog to reach for the dummy. At first help him by holding it in your hand and offering it to him, giving him the command *FETCH* while applying pressure to his teeth, ear, or toe until he opens his mouth. Then insert the dummy.

If he drops the dummy or tries to spit it out, apply pressure and *bump* him with the e-collar. He already knows that when he obeys the command *FETCH* he can avoid discomfort. Each time you offer him the dummy move it down closer to the table. Anytime he doesn't reach for the dummy move it up a little closer to his mouth and continue with the training. Reinforce the command with the e-collar and toe or ear pressure. Keep moving the dummy downward until it is on the table.

Keep going through the process. You want him to get the dummy by himself upon command. Remember, each time he reaches for the dummy and takes it in his mouth, release the pressure and pet him immediately. This is a crucial time. Don't get impatient and be rough with your dog. This training takes patience and time and more time. Once he reaches out and gets the dummy in his mouth when you say FETCH, training will be downhill for both of you.

Reaching, Holding, Walking, Releasing

Now, put all the commands together—he reaches for the dummy, holds it while he is walking, and releases it on command. If he tries to spit the dummy out or drops it, make the correction with the ear key, toe cord, or whatever you are using and the stimulation of the e-collar simultaneously.

After you have completed the initial training to retrieve and before you take your dog to the field, make sure he will hold a bird in his mouth. When you take your dog to the field, put him in full dress—check cord, training collar, and e-collar.

Caution: Be sure you condition your dog to the gun before beginning this training. Don't shoot over him if you've not trained him to the gun. If this is the case, treat him as if he were a gun-shy dog. Follow the procedures in **Chapter 7 – Training in the Field, Preventing Gun-Shyness** and get him conditioned to the gun before you shoot over him.

Take a freshly killed bird and toss it out 6 or 7 feet and fire your gun. You want to see how he will react. If you stand still when you toss out the bird, your dog will do better. Give him the full length of the check-cord and let him go to the bird. In this way you're allowing him to retrieve the bird and bring it back to you, if he is so inclined, without his knowing you have a hold on him. If he brings the bird to you, reward him by petting him.

Dog on check-cord going for a bird

If your dog doesn't go to the bird, take him to it. If he doesn't pick it up, put it in his mouth. Return to where you were standing when you tossed the bird. If he drops the bird or tries to spit it out, correct him with all three prompts. Hold out your hand and say *GIVE*. If you've properly trained him, he should release the bird in your hand. If so, pet him for doing a good job.

If he goes to the bird but doesn't pick it up, tell him *FETCH* and reinforce the command with the stimulation of the e-collar. Keep tossing the bird and firing your gun— gradually increasing the distance you toss it. Continue the training until he will retrieve the freshly killed bird, hold it in his mouth, return to you, and release it on command. Now you're ready to shoot birds over him.

When you shoot a bird over him, go to the bird with him, still keeping him on the check-cord. Let him go to the bird using the full length of the check-cord. If he goes to the bird, picks it up, brings it to you, and releases it on command, you've done well. You're over the hump. After he consistently fetches the bird you've shot while he is on the check-cord, drop the check cord to see what he will do. If his performance is flawless, pet him. If his performance is not flawless, revert to earlier training. Go as far back as needed. With this procedure, you will have a dog you can be proud of—one that will consistently retrieve on command.

Hunting Dogs

If your dog is going to be a hunting dog, let him start going to get the bird when you start killing birds over him. With the check-cord in your hand, take him to the bird. Let him pick up the bird, mouth it if he wants to, and give a little tug on the check-cord and softly say *HERE* after he's got the bird in his mouth. Don't yell. Sometimes you can turn your back on him, and he'll come running to you with the bird because he's afraid you're going to leave him.

Some dogs are just naturally better retrievers than others. Some have to be properly schooled before they will retrieve. Never turn a dog loose to go get the bird until he has been properly trained to retrieve. Always keep him in full dress with the check-cord in hand. Otherwise he may grab the bird and run with it, dig a hole and hide it, or simply just eat it. This creates another problem: He may try to run off with all the birds—thinking they are his. Keep him on the check-cord and continue training him.

Never force break a hunting dog until he has a hunting season behind him. Some dogs that don't like to retrieve *liberated birds*—birds that have been released for training purposes—become good retrievers on wild birds.

CHAPTER 6

USING TRAINING BIRDS

Tethering Pigeons
Launching Pigeons
Flying Quail
Retrieving Quail

The part of the country you live in will determine to a great extent the type of training birds you will use. Pigeons are excellent birds for beginning training. They're readily available, flush easily, put out a lot of scent, and are easily tethered so they won't fly off. Most importantly, they don't have a tendency to crawl under things (as game birds do) where a dog can catch them.

Pigeons are great birds to use when you're teaching your dog to be *steady-to-wing, steady-to-shot, steady-to-kill,* and *stop-to-flush.* After your dog is steady in all these situations, then start using game birds.

If you're running your dog in field trials, train him on the kind of birds to be used in those trials. As a professional field trialer who competes all over the United States and Canada, I train with many different types of birds.

Pigeons

Generally, use pigeons during the early phases of training and begin using game birds when your dog is reliable enough to be turned loose, wearing the check-cord, training collar, and e-collar.

Obtaining and Caring for Pigeons

Wild pigeons are always better than pen-raised ones because they flush better and fly better. Whether you buy pen-raised birds, buy wild birds, or capture your own wild birds, you'll need an enclosure for them. You can build a simple pen out of chicken wire. It doesn't have to be large or fancy—just large enough for you to be able to feed and water the birds. Pigeons are hardy birds and live almost anywhere. Get a manual that tells you how to house, feed, and care for them. Since they put out a lot of scent (they stink), don't put them too close to your house.

Pigeon pen

Controlling Flight and Launching

Controlling the distance a pigeon will fly and eliminating, or at least decreasing, distracting human scent are important elements in training your dog to work birds. The wind conditions and direction affect the way you launch birds. To prevent distracting human scents, the bird needs to be *air washed*. This does not mean the bird has been air washed; it means the human scent has been washed from the bird. A bird is said to be *air washed* when it flies a sufficient distance for the wind to wash away the scent of the person who handled it thereby leaving no human trail scent to the bird.

Tethering

When you're using birds for training, tether them so they can't fly away. Tethered birds not only can't fly away, they can be used over and over.

Note: The tether is a piece of string by which the pigeon is attached to a piece of cardboard so as to limit the distance the bird can fly. Technically speaking, the string is a tether and the cardboard a fetter—something that confines or restrains. Sometimes trainers use the word *tether* to refer to both the tether (string) and the restraint (cardboard).

Keep in mind the fact that some pigeons are stronger fliers than others. A lively bird is usually a strong flier. Size doesn't seem to be a factor. Adjust the size of the cardboard to the bird. Use smaller pieces of cardboard for weak fliers and larger pieces for strong fliers.

Attach the tether to the bird's leg using a slipknot (a knot that slips easily along the cord around which it is made).

Slip knot on pigeon's foot

Use a piece of string or yarn to attach a piece of cardboard to a bird's leg. Brightly colored yarn works well because it is easier to work with, and the bright color of the yarn makes it easier to mark the birds. Use whatever scraps of yarn you have. Pieces of cardboard boxes found at grocery stores, etc., are a good weight for tethering pigeons.

The cardboard should be 5 or 6 inches wide and about 10 inches long. Take a piece of yarn about 15 inches long, double it, and put a knot in one end. Punch a hole in the cardboard about 1 inch from the corner. Put the yarn through the hole and loop it through the end with the knot so the knot on the string will be on the cardboard. Take the other end and put a loop in it and slip it over one of the bird's feet, drawing this slipknot snugly around the bird's leg just above the foot.

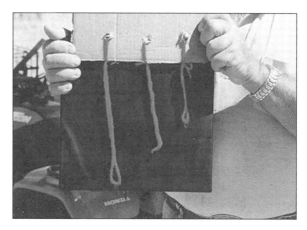

Long, average, and short tethers

Matching Tether and Cover

In shorter cover, use longer strings. In taller cover, use shorter strings—the shorter the better. You don't want the string to hang up in the cover when the bird flushes. Be sure to tie a strong, sturdy knot; otherwise, the bird may dislodge the string from the cardboard and fly away.

After you've correctly attached the cardboard to the bird's leg, it's ready to be *flown out* (launched). *Fly out* a bird by tossing it in the air. If you want it to fly a greater distance, toss it up in the air. If you want it to fly a shorter distance, toss it close to the ground in the direction you want it to go.

Trainer removing flight feathers to limit flying distance

If it's a strong bird or there's quite a bit of wind (*see* **Appendix 3 – Beaufort Scale**), you may want to pull out a couple of flight feathers (also called greater primary coverts) from one side. If you pull feathers from both sides, he will still be balanced and able to fly away.

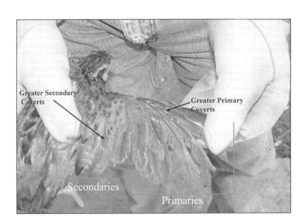

Quail with primary and secondary coverts marked

Dizzy (also called *rocking*) a bird by grasping the back of its body with one hand (unless you have small hands), firmly holding the wings close to its body and twirling it around a few times—using just wrist motion—not your arm. You're just making the bird a little dizzy, not practicing to become a pitcher for the Giants. Don't put the bird's head under his wing. If you do he will not get up and fly naturally. Don't plant the bird under a bush or other cover. Just toss it out.

The best training is done when you do absolutely nothing to the bird—except tether it—and let it fly out naturally.

Grasping a pigeon   **Dizzy pigeon**

Training in Confined Area

If your training area has limited space, you may still train with pigeons. Use heavier restraints (pieces of cardboard) so the birds can't fly very far. People who work with homing pigeons use bird launchers. After these birds are released, they fly home.

Bird Launcher

Others who have limited training space *dizzy* their birds, tuck the bird's head under its wing, and plant it under cover. Neither of these alternatives are good ones because human scent is intense in both. You don't want your dog to follow human scent to find birds. You want him to find birds by picking up their scent.

Bobwhite Quail

Although I train with other liberated game birds—chukars, pheasants, Hungarian partridges (Huns), and quail—I prefer working with bobwhite quail. They're the most widely used field trial birds in the United States. They won't run as much or fly as far as other game birds, but they're similar to other game birds in that they put out scent and hide in cover.

Bobwhites are easy to raise and can be used over and over because they are covey birds—birds that keep together, feed together, and regroup after being disturbed. When used as training birds, they will return to the pen (a call-back pen or johnny house) from which they were flown out.

Call-back pen

You may raise your own quail, or you may buy them from game bird farms. They're easy to care for. Just keep them dry, fed, and watered. A call-back pen 8 feet long, 4 feet wide, and 2 feet high is a good size. Use wood for half of the enclosure and put a roof over it. Use wire for the other half of the structure. Put a door on the front for flying out birds and put a door on the top for feeding and watering them. Put a re-entry funnel at the bottom of the pen. Use a standard bird watering dish and keep it clean and free of algae. Feed game bird feed to your quail.

Don't fly your birds out until you've conditioned them to come back to the pen. Let the birds walk out of the pen several times. Don't flush them. They'll walk around and then learn to go back to the pen where their food is. When you begin flying birds out of the pen, leave one or more birds in the pen to act as *call-back* birds. They'll begin to call, and the birds that have walked or flown out will come back to the pen—re-entering through the specially designed funnel at the bottom of the pen. After being flown out of the pen several times, bobwhite quail come back to it whether there is a *call-back* bird in the pen or not.

Re-entry hole in call-back pen

You may also use a battery operated *call-back* bird. This highly effective device comes with complete directions for use and placement.

Mechanical call-back bird

CHAPTER 7

TRAINING IN THE FIELD

Chasing Birds
Gun-Shyness
Running at Birds
Steady-to-Wing
Steady-to-Wing-and-Shot
Steady-to-Wing-Shot-and-Kill
Steady-to-Wing-Shot-Kill-and-Retrieve
Relocating
Stop-to-Flush
Honoring

Beginning Bird Work

You're now ready to introduce your dog to bird work and all it entails. For a great hunter or a field trial champion, the training you do now is critical. You want to train your dog to be *steady-to-wing, steady-to-wing-and-shot, steady-to-wing-shot-and-kill,* and *steady-to-wing-shot-kill-and-retrieve*.

You don't want to create problems—such as gun-shyness, flagging, creeping, or busting birds. If some of these problems have been created, correct them before moving on. *See* **Chapter 8 – Correcting Behavior Problems**.

Letting Your Dog Chase Birds

First, take your dog to the field and have fun with him. If he's large enough to wear a training collar, put one on him and attach a check-cord to it. If he's too small to wear a training collar, attach the check-cord to his ID collar. If you have the ideal condition—a field where he can chase birds—let him have fun chasing them, dragging an unattended check-cord. (A check-cord is *unattended* when you don't have it in your hand.)

If he catches a bird, that's fine. Catching birds will arouse his interest. If there are no birds in the field or you have limited space, put some birds out for him to find and chase. Tethered pigeons work well. Two things are happening here: He's getting interested in birds, and he's getting accustomed to dragging the check-cord—an important aspect of future training.

Preventing Gun-Shyness

You want to introduce your dog to gunfire in such a way that he will not become gun-shy. After your dog has become sufficiently fired up about chasing birds—at least two or three sessions in the field—let him continue to chase birds, still dragging his unattended check-cord.

When he gets out a little ways—30 or 40 feet chasing a bird—fire your gun, using a low caliber gun such as a .22 caliber starter pistol. Don't fire right over him. Put the pistol down behind you and fire or just hold the pistol in the air and fire.

Pay close attention to your dog. If he stops, or if he stops and comes back to you, let him chase more birds before you fire again. Once you've let him chase birds and he shows no sign of being frightened by the sound of the gun, you've probably done a good job introducing your dog to birds and gunfire without his becoming gun shy.

Letting Your Dog Run at Birds

After a few bird-chasing sessions in which he drags an unattended check-cord, put him in full dress—training collar, check-cord, and e-collar. Put the e-collar on him, but don't use it at this time. You just want him to get accustomed to having it on whenever he's in training.

With the training collar on your dog and the check-cord in your hand, let him run at birds—pigeons you have tethered with a string attached to a piece of cardboard.

When your dog points a bird, walk past him and flush it. More than likely he'll run past you and try to catch it.

Remember, catching birds is a natural bird dog instinct. They survived by hunting, catching, and eating birds long before people began training them to hunt birds to put meat on the table.

Never let your dog catch the bird. *Circle* him. (*Circle* is just a term for the procedure.) You're not going to move your dog in a complete circle (360 degrees). To *circle* him, step to one side and use the check-cord to move him in a circular manner so he ends up near you on a loose lead. Never let him hit the end of the check-cord. Keep him on a loose lead and pet him while he watches the bird fly away.

"Circling" a dog

In this *circling* process, you will be using the momentum of the dog to help you move him in a semi-circle. If you do not step to the side, you'll have to jerk on the check-cord and will be unable to bring him to your side. This is a simple procedure, although some people have difficulty grasping the idea and executing the maneuver.

The more aggressively your dog runs at birds, the better the training will be. For very aggressive dogs, sometimes this feat is difficult to accomplish, so be as careful as possible with an aggressive dog. Some seemingly aggressive dogs are not as tough as they appear to be and will quit pointing birds. If this happens, you'll have to rekindle his interest in birds.

Steady-to-Wing

Steady-to-Wing is also called *broke-to-wing*. Your dog is *steady-to-wing* when he *stands-up-stands-still* when you go in front of him and flush a bird. While you're teaching your dog to be *steady-to-wing*, never shoot over him. Complete this training to the point that he always allows you to pass him and flush the bird. You definitely do not want to shoot over him unless you've over-trained him and created a problem. *See* **Chapter 8 – Correcting Behavior Problems**.

You'll probably have to work your dog many times before he's ready to work birds. Remember to use very low levels of stimulation. You may find you'll have to go back to using just the training collar and check-cord to work him on birds. If you have to go back to earlier training, leave the e-collar on him but don't use it. So much of bird dog training is a forwards and backwards process. Sometimes you may feel you're taking one step forward and two steps back. However, this forwards and backwards procedure is the best way of training with the e-collar.

Continue letting him run at birds and *circling* him. Now begin using the stimulation of the e-collar in conjunction with the training collar and the check-cord when he runs at a bird. When he rushes the bird, *circle* him and simultaneously *bump* him with a low level of stimulation from the e-collar. You're now beginning to teach him to *respect* birds and to stay on point. While you're training your dog on birds, use the e-collar in conjunction with the training collar and check-cord, but do not use the e-collar alone. *See* **Chapter 3 – Collars, Training Collar and Check-Cord, and E-collar**.

Often birds will run—especially when you start working your dog on wild birds. When a bird runs, use the same techniques you use when you want him to stop. *See* **Chapter 4 – Teaching Basic Commands,** *Stop-Stand-Up-Stand-Still*.

As you start setting these fundamental hunting skills, the age of the dog has little bearing on the success of the training. It's the level of maturity—not the chronological age—that's important. Never say *WHOA* during this training. In fact, say nothing to your dog. Often people talk to their dog and are unaware of it. If you think you may be inclined to unconsciously talk to your dog, put duct tape over your mouth. Some people who watch my training videos use the duct tape, but few admit it. If you talk to your dog, you'll reduce your chances of successfully training him to be *steady-to-wing* and weaken subsequent training based on this skill.

Duct tape deterrent for unconscious talking

Flying Birds Over Your Dog

At first, flush birds away from your dog. Then, as he begins to stand on his own and progresses in his training as you're using the e-collar, fly birds over him. You need to be very careful at this time because you can cause him to not want to point a bird. Let him continue to run at birds, but don't let him catch them.

At this early stage of training your dog on birds, use the e-collar in conjunction with the training collar and check-cord. Do not use the e-collar alone. *See* **Chapter 3 – Collars, Training Collar and Check-Cord, and Electronic Collar**.

Your dog, not you, will decide when it is time for him to stop running at birds. The time varies from dog to dog. Some dogs will stop running at birds in three days; some will stop in three weeks; and, well, some dogs will stop only after a much longer period of time.

Be patient. The more frequently you work your dog, the faster he will learn and retain what he has been taught. I work dogs every day, and if some of them have trouble learning, I work them twice a day during this crucial bird working period. Read your own dog. Don't be guided by some other dog's temperament or timetable.

Never try to stop your dog from running at birds until he respects them. If you do, he may start "blinking birds." A dog is blinking a bird when he scents it and leaves. He's pretending he didn't scent it.

Your job is to help him learn to respect birds by moving to a higher level of stimulation appropriate for your dog. By this time you should know the level of stimulation appropriate for your dog. You will not use as much stimulation at this time as you may in later training. This is the time when many handlers use too much e-collar too soon. Not only do you want to train your dog to respect birds that you flush, you want him to be steady when a bird runs rather than flushes.

When your dog has learned to *stop-stand-up-stand-still* and to let you get out in front of him, he's ready for a more advanced lesson. When you take your dog to a bird, he'll *stop-stand-up-stand-still*; however, the scent of the bird will probably be so tempting he may want to lunge at it. By now you'll be working him with the e-collar only, but he's still wearing his training collar and dragging the unattended check-cord.

When he picks up his foot, indicating he's going to move, *bump* him with the e-collar as he starts to move, but do not utter a sound. Do not—I repeat—do not wait until he puts his foot down before you make the correction. Instantly *bump* him, reinforcing his nonverbal WHOA or *stand-up-stand-still* training. If you *bump* him after he puts his foot down, he'll think he's being reprimanded for putting his foot down—not for moving. Praise him by petting him after you've flushed the bird and he *stands*. At this time, continue practicing flushing using the same method over and over.

With practice, your dog will put all the elements together. He'll let you know when he's ready to stop running at birds—by showing he respects them. He respects the bird when he (1) stops, (2) *stands-up-stands-still*, (3) lets you get out in front of him and flush the bird, and (4) waits for you to come back and pet him while you and he watch the bird fly away. When this happens, he has mastered his first basic hunting skill.

When possible, do all your yard work in the field around birds and in between birds. If your dog makes a mistake during the training, correct him and move on. Give him a good experience—find a bird, shoot it for him, and feed part or all of it to him—and put him in his kennel in a good frame of mind.

Note: You may have to teach your dog to eat the bird or part of it after you've removed the feathers. If he's reluctant to eat the bird, take him to the field hungry. Sometimes I snap off the feet of the bird and let the dog have them. You may have to hold these "Feetos" in the side of your dog's mouth to encourage him to chew on them. Once a dog starts chewing on them, he likes the taste and the crunchy sound. Some people think this training encourages a dog to chew on birds or eat them on his own. This is incorrect thinking. This training will encourage him to bring birds to you and get a reward. It does not encourage him to eat birds on his own.

Rekindling Interest in Birds

At any time during training, if your dog shows signs of losing interest in birds—dropping his tail, turning sideways and looking at you, not exhibiting his normal stylish pointing—you're pushing him too fast.

Don't talk to your dog or raise the level of stimulation of the e-collar too much. If you do, your dog will lose interest in the training. If this is the case, shoot a bird for him and then put him in his crate or kennel. The more birds you shoot for him the more you will kindle his interest in birds resulting in better and quicker training.

The first thing you need to do when you introduce him to birds is treat him as if he is gun-shy. *See* **Preventing Gun-Shyness** in this chapter. Resume this training in the next session. In this way you can keep him excited about birds.

The next time you bring your dog out, immediately put him on a bird and shoot it for him before you do any other type of training. No matter what he does you can always go back and practice and reinforce earlier training. Remember, you must always rekindle his interest in birds before further training.

The training you do now depends upon your dog's interest. Again, you may need to shoot another bird over him just as you did the last time you worked him. Do so and then put him in his crate or kennel. You may need to revert to some of the training that you were doing when you first began teaching him to be *steady-to-wing*.

Steady-to-Wing Reliability

Continue training until you're sure he knows to *stop-stand-up-stand-still* between birds. You may have to repeat the process over and over. There is no magic time. Your dog must *stand*, let you flush a bird, and then stay put while you pet him on a loose lead as the bird flies away. This is the first bird dog hunting skill

Remember: Do not say *WHOA* or *GOOD BOY* or anything else to your dog at this time. Repeat this process many times. Reliability is what you're looking for—a dog that is *steady-to-wing* every time you take him out where birds are.

Your dog is *steady-to-wing* when you can flush birds—not only away from him—but over him, under him, and all around him—and he does not move, and you can go back and pet him—still keeping silent. He should also stand and point a bird that is running—not try to chase it. When you test to see if he's *broke-to-wing*, and you're thinking about moving to *broke-to-wing-and-shot* training, make sure you've conditioned him to the e-collar. He's now ready to be shot over.

Steady-to-Wing-and-Shot

Now, start teaching your dog to be *steady-to-wing-and-shot*—the second bird dog hunting skill. Your dog should be wearing his training collar, e-collar, be dragging the check-cord, and getting out away from you.

Start using your shotgun. Sometime you may have to revert to the *steady-to-wing* lesson. Often a dog will stand and let the bird fly but comes unglued when you fire over him. If this is the case, go back to the *steady-to-wing* training—perhaps one or two lessons—to be sure he is completely conditioned to the e-collar.

Flushing Birds and Firing a Gun

The process of *breaking-to-wing-and-shot* is a test of training you did in the past. At first, flush birds away from him and fire your gun. As he progresses in his training, fly birds over him and fire your gun. Use the same procedures as you did teaching him to be *steady-to-wing*. When you fire over him, you want to be in position with the e-collar. (He's still wearing the training collar and dragging the check-cord.) You're introducing him to something he hasn't done before. If he moves, stop him with stimulation of the e-collar. He has already been trained to be *steady-to-wing*.

Making Corrections

If you've done a good job teaching him to be *steady-to-wing*, he will need very little electrical stimulation for corrections. If he is not responsive to the low level of stimulation, use the training collar and check-cord to spin him around for correction. Get out in front of him as if you are flushing and then go back and pet him. If he moves when you fire your gun, use the e-collar to stop him, increasing the level of stimulation very slightly. When you're using the e-collar, always increase the levels of stimulation gradually. Use only enough force to get the desired response.

You're not killing the bird at this time. You're just firing your gun. You're training him to be *steady-to-wing-and-shot.* However, if he acts like he's losing interest, rekindle it by shooting a bird for him. Go to the bird with him and let him do with the bird whatever he wants to do. Then put him in his crate or kennel. You may have to shift back and forth between *steady-to-wing* and *steady-to-shot.* Continue this training in as many sessions as needed until he consistently stands still for *flush-and-shot.*

Steady-to-Wing-Shot-and-Kill

After you're satisfied your dog is *steady-to-wing-and-shot* (you can shoot a shotgun when you flush a bird over him, he consistently stands still and shows no fear of the e-collar), it's time to begin training him to be *steady-to-wing-shot-and-kill*—the third bird dog hunting skill.

Use the same procedures you used in training him to be *steady-to-wing-and-shot.* Start him out by flying birds away from him. Be sure you're ready with the e-collar when you use your shotgun to shoot his first bird. (He's still wearing the training collar and dragging the check-cord.) The bird must be flying away from him when you kill it. If it goes back over him or by him, do not shoot it—shoot in the air and let the bird fly away, keeping him *steady-to-wing-and-shot*.

Repeat the process of killing a bird flying away from him. At this time, your dog should be broke enough to allow you to go get the bird and bring it back while he is still standing. When he has reached this stage of the training, he is ready for you to begin putting more pressure on him by killing birds that are flying over him. Never shoot birds if the conditions might endanger your dog. If your dog tries to go for the bird, correct him with the e-collar. He may not be ready for being *steady-to-kill*, and if he isn't, go back to *steady-to-shot* training. He must stay on point.

If you've religiously followed the foregoing procedures when training your dog to be *steady-to-wing-and-shot*, you shouldn't have any problems at this time, but all dogs are different. You have to adjust your training to your particular dog. If your dog shows any signs of losing interest, go back to *steady-to-wing-and-shot* or even *steady-to-wing*. He must be reliably consistent in these basic skills before you teach to be *steady-to-wing-shot-and-kill*. Take him back as far as you need to rekindle his interest. Killing birds for him will definitely rekindle his interest. Don't let him go get the bird at this time unless he indicates he is losing interest in birds.

Remember, do this training without saying a word. I cannot stress often enough how important it is for you **to not give any verbal commands to your dog during this training**. Continue this training until he is consistently reliable— points a bird and stands through the flush, the shot, the kill, and you go get the bird for him.

Steady-to-Wing-Shot-Kill-and-Retrieve

After you're satisfied your dog is *steady-to-wing-shot-and-kill* (he consistently stays rigidly on point as you flush and shoot birds over him), you may want to move him to the fourth bird dog hunting skill—*steady-to-wing-shot-kill-*

and-retrieve. To teach your dog this skill, *see* **Chapter 5 – Teaching Your Dog to Retrieve**. Use the sections that are applicable to your dog and what you want him to do.

Turning Your Dog Loose on Birds

Once you get your dog trained to *wing-shot-and-kill* and he stops on command, gradually let him get out farther dragging the check-cord. When all this comes together, he'll *stand a bird*, let you flush it, kill it, and continue to *stand* until you get the bird and bring it back—without your giving any verbal commands.

If he gets out too far and you are forced to use the e-collar too often, he'll lose interest because he's tired of being chastised. Anytime he loses interest when he is to the fore, repeat the training at a closer range.

Up to this point, your dog has been in full dress (training collar, check-cord, and e-collar) when you were walking him—handling at any distance. Now, you're going to turn him loose, wearing only the e-collar. First, work him at a close range going through all the commands he has learned. Gradually, increase his range. If he doesn't respond appropriately to a command, shorten his range and start over.

This is a critical time. Be patient. Don't rush your dog. Again, this training may take a day, perhaps a week, a month, or even longer, depending on your dog's temperament and how consistent and regularly you work him. The more regularly you work him the longer he will retain the lesson. Be sure he is steady in one phase before you introduce him to a new one.

When he reaches the limit of the range you were working him when he was wearing full dress, you've done well with his training. This indicates he is trustworthy at any range and ready for future training with only the electric collar.

Relocating Your Dog

When your dog goes on point and you're unable to produce the bird, relocate him. You want him to either locate the bird that you can't find or to move on and continue hunting. To relocate your dog, give him a nonverbal command—a tap on the side or a little toot on a whistle—or a one-word verbal command such as *okay*. Whatever command you use, be consistent. This is a command you will use anytime you want to release him.

Your dog will enjoy a pat on the side. He will like the feel of your hand on him. The little pat not only releases him, it makes him understand that he's doing a good job. It is almost like a quick petting.

You want to teach your dog to let **you** relocate **him**—not relocate himself. When he points a bird, give him the signal to relocate after you've made an effort to flush. Even though you know where the bird is, continue to give him this signal until he flushes it. Use the stimulation of the e-collar to make the correction as soon as the bird flushes. You may also want to spin him at this time. He's ready for this correction because he has already been fully conditioned to the e-collar and associates the correction with his action. In this way he learns not to relocate on his own. He thinks he's doing the relocating and learns self-relocation is not a good thing.

Stop-to-Flush

Stop-to-flush occurs when a dog runs over a bird he has not scented or sighted, flushes it, stops as if he is on point, and stays there until his handler releases him. Flushing a bird in this manner is not the same as *bumping* a bird. A dog *bumps* a bird intentionally. He scents the bird and continues moving until he flushes it. Sometimes he will point a bird and then move, but on the way he *bumps* it.

Be alert. Be ready with the e-collar. Have your finger on

102

the button of the e-collar transmitter. Make the correction immediately. If you're fumbling around trying to find your transmitter, you can't make the necessary instantaneous correction.

Teach your dog to *stop-to-flush* after you've broken him to *wing-and-shot*. Turn your dog loose. When he runs over a bird and the bird flushes and he doesn't stop, then you stop him instantly with the stimulation of the e-collar. You may be tempted to give him a verbal command such as *WHOA*. Don't do it. **DO NOT SAY ANYTHING**.

Approach him and *spin* him around to let him know you're displeased with what he has just done. Do not take him back to where he flushed the bird. Returning to the scene of the crime may work for human beings, but dogs don't understand it. It makes no sense to them. The appropriate correction is to spin him right where he is. After a few sessions, he'll begin to consistently *stop-to-flush*. In between the *stop-to-flush* activity, fly some pigeons over him to reinforce the idea that when a bird is in the air he is to stop as if he is on point.

Spinning a dog for correction

Stop-to-flush is imperative for a field trial dog, but it is also an asset in a hunting dog. While hunting, if your dog flushes a bird and is trained to *stop-to-flush*, you'll have a chance to approach your dog, flush the birds still there, and bag a few.

Honoring

At the same time you're training your dog to be *steady-to-wing-shot-and-kill* begin teaching him to respect other dogs by *honoring (backing)* them when they're on point.

When one dog sees another dog or dogs on point, he must stop and look like he's on point, but actually he is recognizing the dog on point. This situation is called *backing* or *honoring*. The term *backing* suggests the second dog is confirming the first dog's point. However, some people are misled by this term, thinking *backing* occurs in back of the first dog.

The term *honoring* is less confusing and more descriptive of the act. A dog can *honor* another dog from any position, not just in back of the pointing dog. *Honoring* is important in both hunting and field trialing because dogs should not interfere with other dogs on point.

If you're hunting and your dog *steals point* (goes past dog on point and then goes on point between first dog and the bird), your hunting partners will not be happy with you, and you may find yourself hunting alone. Furthermore, some dogs simply will not tolerate another dog *stealing point* and will fight with any dog that tries to do so. If they get into a fight, the dog who *steals point* is at fault.

If you're field trialing your dog in a *broke dog* stake and he *steals point*, he'll be disqualified—if the judge sees him.

Teaching your dog to *honor* is one of the easiest parts of your training. Your dog should at least be *steady-to-wing* when you start teaching him to *honor* and *steady-to-wing-and-shot* when you start using the e-collar by itself.

When another dog is on point and your dog approaches and sees the other dog, immediately stop him, using the same method you used when you were teaching him to *stand-up-stand-still*—flip the check-cord to make a noise at the training collar buckle. If your dog doesn't stop on the nonverbal command in response to the flip of the check-cord and training collar, reinforce the command with stimulation of the e-collar.

Do not use verbal commands. If you use a verbal command at this point, your dog may become confused—not knowing what you want him to do—and start *blinking* dogs on point (that is, leaving the area or running off).

Continue to use the check-cord, training collar, and e-collar. After your training has advanced to *shot*, and your dog has more e-collar training, you may then use only the e-collar.

Do not remove the training collar and the check-cord. Keep them on him, but don't use them. Your dog must continue to stand while the bird is being flushed in front of the pointing dog. When he moves, stop him with the e-collar, go to him, and spin him. Continue to stop him with the e-collar and spin him until he is reliable—that is, when he consistently stops when he sees another dog on point and stands until the bird is flushed. Then you no longer have to use the e-collar.

Pointer on point and Brittany honoring

Honoring a Silhouette

If you don't have a broke dog to help teach your dog to honor, use a silhouette of a dog. Sometimes using a silhouette works better than using another dog because you can place it closer to the bird before your dog sees it. You may put the silhouette behind a bush, behind a mound, in a ditch, and so forth. In this way you can work your dog at your desired range before he sees the artificial dog on point.

You can buy a silhouette of a dog from a sporting goods store, or if you're handy with a saw you may make your own and paint it to look like a dog.

Before you take your dog out to train, put the silhouette in a place that will not allow your dog to see it until he gets within a normal range. Some dogs will honor at a greater range, but the normal range for a dog to honor is about 15 to 40 feet. Next, put a bird in front of the silhouette. Take your dog out of his crate or kennel. Be sure he is wearing full dress (training collar, check-cord, and e-collar). Use the same techniques discussed above.

The silhouette never takes the place of a real dog on point. Eventually, you'll need to teach your dog to honor another dog. Try to get a friend who has a broke dog to train with you or borrow a broke dog.

Pointer honoring a silhouette

Working Edges

Edges are transitional zones such as fence rows, ravines, roads, brush lines, timber lines, and so forth, and game birds frequently hide in the cover offered by these areas. Before you begin teaching your dog to run edges, he should be at least *steady-to-wing*—preferably *steady-to-wing-and-shot*. If he is not at least *steady-to-wing*, you won't be able to flush birds over him without his chasing them back into the thicket and possibly getting lost. If he's *steady-to-wing-and-shot,* you can shoot over him, and he will be more enthusiastic about hunting the edges.

Some hunters and handlers refer to this work as *running edges*, and others refer to it as *working edges*. Use the term you prefer.

To teach your dog to run *edges*, you'll need to run him or road him, handling him at close range. You can do this training either on foot or on horseback. Basically, teaching a dog to run *edges* is similar to teaching him to *pattern*. However, in this training, you need to put birds out along the edges where you are roading or running him.

When you're working him on foot keep him at a closer range. Whether you're working him on foot or on horseback, you'll need to put him on an edge where there are birds and give him a nonverbal command to go forward (using whatever command you use to release him). I like to tap the dog on the side to release him and let him know I want him to go forward and hunt. Any time he gets off the edge, immediately stop him with a nonverbal command *(stop-stand-up-stand-still)* and start him over with a nonverbal release command. Don't let him get off the edge. After he finds a few birds on the edges, he'll not have to be encouraged to hunt them. He knows he can find birds there.

The rewards of a well-trained bird dog

CHAPTER 8

CORRECTING BEHAVIOR PROBLEMS

Problems
Solutions
Prevention

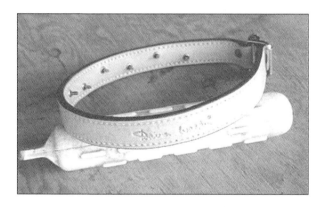

Fear is the cause of many common behavior problems. Dogs, like many people, are afraid of new things, new places, or new situations. Bold people are not intimidated by new situations. Shy or timid people are often frightened by change or by unfamiliar conditions. Read your dog just as you read people when you're trying to understand where they're coming from, what their motivation is, and why they act the way they do. *See* **Chapter 2 – Starting Your Pup, Reading Your Dog's Body Language**. Where is he coming from? What is the source of his problem? Why is he acting the way he is?

109

Do not Return to the Scene of the Crime. A common misconception is the belief that a dog must be returned to the scene of his crime for correction. This concept probably comes from child psychology. The thought behind it is that unless children are returned to the place where they erred, they will not know why they're being corrected. This theory may or may not hold true for children, but it definitely doesn't for dogs.

With a dog, immediacy is the key. He associates any correction with the present time. If you take him back to the place where he made an incorrect response, he may think you're taking him for a friendly little walk and will be happy to go with you and doesn't understand why you're punishing him.

All too often a trainer will attempt to take a dog back to the place where he made his mistake. The trainer more than likely will not go back to the exact spot, and the dog certainly doesn't know where it is. He doesn't even know what he did wrong.

Make an immediate correction at the time of the misdeed by picking your dog up by his collar—just high enough for his front legs to clear the ground—and *spin* him 360 degrees.

He doesn't enjoy this *spin*. It doesn't hurt him, but it lets him know he's not performing in an acceptable manner. Some old-line trainers believed a good thrashing was the only way to correct a dog. A *spin* gets the same result as a thrashing; furthermore, he will want to avoid doing whatever he did to cause the *spin*.

Note: If your dog is heavy and you have difficulty spinning him with his feet just slightly off the ground, solve the problem by lifting his front a little higher. This extra height will enable you to *spin* him more easily. The *spin* is governed by your strength and the size of your dog.

If your dog continues to make the same mistakes or makes a very serious mistake, do a more stringent correction by increasing the intensity of the *spin*. About half-way through the spin (when he's behind you at about 180 degrees) give the check-cord a couple of quick jerks without stopping the spin. He dislikes this jerking motion even more than he dislikes the *spinning*. When you do this, he will know he has done wrong because you're displeased with his conduct.

Barking Excessively

Problem: Barking without a reason other than simply to get attention. Often dogs bark because they're insecure or lonely. They're not accustomed to being left alone in a kennel. It doesn't matter whether you have one dog or a dozen dogs in your kennel. They just don't like to be left alone, especially if they are accustomed to spending their nights in the house with the family.

When you leave them in the kennel, they'll bark at other animals: dogs, horses, cows, or any visiting wild animals such as coons. They bark at night, but they also bark during the day. Sometimes dogs will bark just for the fun of barking. They like to hear their own voice. Often dogs bark because they are bored. They're trying to tell you they would like to be taken out and exercised. Whatever the reason for the barking, it is annoying and should not be tolerated.

Solution: In the past if a dog barked excessively, owners used a variety of methods to shut him up. Some would sneak up and throw water on him. Others would hide and shoot him with a BB gun. Others used more severe types of correction that were effective but potentially harmful. With the advent of the *bark collar,* such harsh corrections are no longer necessary.

Today, you can effectively and efficiently stop a dog from barking without harming him. You simply put a *bark collar* on him. A *bark collar* is a self-activating collar that delivers a low level of electrical stimulation when the dog barks. Some models can be adjusted to the temperament of a particular dog. This adjustment is important if your dog has a sensitive nature. These collars come with simple instructions. Tri-tronic™ makes a very dependable one. *See* **Appendix 4 – Useful Names and Addresses**.

Blinking Birds

Problem: A dog leaves a point before the handler reaches him. This is a man-made problem. Overzealous training in the presence of birds is usually the cause. Blinking a bird takes different forms. A dog may establish point and leave. He may partially establish point and fade. He may ignore the bird after he smells it. In all three situations, he seems to be saying, "What, me smell a bird? I don't smell anything."

Blinking birds and being gun-shy are the two most common and most serious bird dog problems, and they often go together. A blinking dog is a scared dog. He's afraid of birds, and he is probably afraid of guns. He may even fear his handler if he was harshly handled when he was being worked on birds. A dog blinks birds because he has been mishandled or abused around birds. I don't mean he has been physically beaten. I mean a handler has unwittingly sent him the wrong message—verbal *WHOAING* and other types of over-handling, such as being bumped with the e-collar when he hasn't been properly conditioned to it. He becomes frightened and confused. When your dog is around birds and you talk to him and use the e-collar at the same time, more than likely he'll *blink* birds.

If a dog has been mistreated elsewhere, he becomes frightened of everything—whether he's at home or in the field. Although overzealous training in the presence of birds is usually the culprit, it isn't the only cause of blinking.

Anything that makes him uncomfortable in the presence of birds can lead to blinking. It may be the physical conditions of the terrain such as sharp rocks or sand spurs.

Solution: When you're working your dog on a bird and he's running at the bird, don't let him reach the end of the check-cord. Dogs—as do people—experience pain when they "reach the end of their rope." If you let him reach the end of the check-cord, he'll experience pain and will associate it with the bird. *See* **Chapter 7 – Training in the Field, Introducing Your Dog to Bird Work**.

If the blinking is caused by the terrain, put dog boots on him. Boots will protect his feet, and he'll not associate his discomfort with the birds.

Dog boots

Prevention: Be extremely careful when you begin working your dog on birds. Don't over-handle him. Don't correct him for something until you are absolutely certain he understands why you're correcting him. Never use the e-collar without the check-cord and training collar until you've conditioned him to the feel of it.

Bolting *See* **Running Away**

Bumping or Busting Birds

Problem: A dog flushes a bird on his own. After dogs are broke, they may revert to bumping birds when they are lost or get out away from you. Sometimes they start flushing birds on their own when they're out of sight because they like to see the birds in the air, and you're not there to stop them.

Frequently, they will begin bumping birds when they've been on point too long or when they see the bird— whether it is running or staying still. After they've bumped a few birds on their own, they begin to like it. How long is *too long*? Know your dog. For some dogs a few minutes is too long. For others an hour is too long.

Solution: To correct this problem, you have to go back and retrain, starting at ground zero. Walk him on the check-cord. Stop him. Get out in front of him. Since he's a trained dog, if he moves when the bird gets up, stop him with the e-collar and be more aggressive when you *spin* him. Let him stand on point longer. Flush birds back towards him when possible. This will put more stress on him, and he will soon learn you want him to *stand-a-bird* until you get to him.

Be ready with the e-collar at all times. Hide and watch him for a while so you can catch him in the act of moving and flushing a bird. Immediately bump him with the e-collar and go to him and *spin* him aggressively.

Continue this training until he is reliable: He will then *stand* and not *bump* a bird when he is out on his own. Since he has already been through the breaking process, this time you will want to be more aggressive in your training. *See* **Chapter 7 – Training in the Field**, *Steady-to-Wing-and-Shot*.

Prevention: You've already trained your dog to be *steady-to-wing-and-shot*, and if he begins to bump birds, you are probably responsible. You may need to be more attentive. Don't let him get into situations where he'll be tempted to take a bird out. Use more aggressive handling to keep him in close range until he is absolutely reliable. Don't be lax.

Cat-Walking

Problem: A dog establishes point or almost establishes point and begins to try to sneak up on the bird. This sneaky walking is called *cat-walking* or *creeping*. This behavior is a man-made problem and can be avoided by not talking to the dog when he is being trained to *respect* birds. Often this problem occurs when a dog is being trained to be *steady-to-wing*.

A creeping dog wants to either catch or flush the bird— whichever comes first. He has not been taught to respect the bird. Many things tempt him to creep—birds planted in such a manner that he can catch them or birds having human scent on them because they've been dizzied and planted under a bush or put in a bird thrower.

Often he is confused by his handler who is trying to help him point by continually saying *WHOOP, WHOA,* or whatever he thinks will help the dog become steady on the bird. If the dog is a pointing dog, he does not need help in pointing birds. He does it instinctively, and any command he gets while he's trying to point birds will confuse him.

Solution: Never talk to your dog when he is on point or trying to point. Quit saying all those commands *WHOOP, WHOA, STEADY BOY,* and so forth. Don't use bird throwers or dizzy birds and put them under bushes. These birds carry human scent and will cause your dog to feel he can catch the bird, and he probably can. Go back to the basics and walk him between birds. Teach him to *stand-up-stand-still* and to let you get out in front of him. If he has already been conditioned to the e-collar, make the corrections with it.

Chasing Trash

Problem: The most common trash (non-game birds and animals) is small birds, commonly called dickeybirds. (Any small birds may be called dickeybirds.) Generally, dogs that chase non-game birds and fur-bearing animals are so full of energy they have to chase something—dickeybirds, skunks, porcupines, deer, and so forth.

Chasing trash is often bred into dogs, and some lines are worse than others. I've had many dogs that improved the breed—their *get* (progeny) were better bird dogs than they were—but they would also chase dickeybirds or any type of fur-bearing animal. They were not particular; they'd chase anything that moved. Perhaps this chasing instinct comes from having some hound in them from long ago.

Solution: This minor problem is easily corrected. Use the e-collar; however, before you use the e-collar to stop your dog from chasing trash, be sure you have properly conditioned him to the feel of it. *See* **Chapter 3 – Collars, Electronic Collar**. Some dogs will need to be broke from chasing trash at a very young age, so be careful when you use the e-collar. You could get your dog to where he won't point any birds. This happens often. The problem is caused by a handler not knowing how to use the e-collar correctly.

Chasing Dickeybirds Solution: When he's interested in dickeybirds, don't say anything to him. Wait until he gets up real close to the bird, so close you are positive he knows the reason for the correction. *Bump* him with low stimulation. Keep *bumping* him. You'll see him begin to slow down. The trick is to get him to learn the difference between dickeybirds (which he must ignore) and game birds (which he must point).

If he starts pointing dickeybirds, keep up the training—but with lower level stimulation until he stands and watches them fly away. Gradually, keep raising the level of stimulation. (If you *bump* him with too much stimulation, he may run away from the bird instead of stopping.) A dog may start *blinking* game birds when his handler is too hard on him with the e-collar when he's interested in dickeybirds.

Continue the training. It is better to *bump* him with lower level three or four times before you go to a higher level. He will think the dickeybird is causing his discomfort. Eventually, he will slow down and watch the dickeybirds fly away. When he does this, he will then begin to ignore dickeybirds because he has learned if he ignores them, he can avoid discomfort.

Chasing Fur-bearing Animals Solution: To stop your dog from chasing fur-bearing animals, particularly deer, use the same procedures you used to stop him from chasing dickeybirds. However, use them more intensely because you don't care if he runs away from the animals; in fact, you want him to run away from them because they can hurt him.

Chasing Vehicles

Problem: Most dogs do not chase vehicles. Some dogs chase vehicles probably because they are bored. They are having fun running and chasing something that's trying to get away from them. It's just a matter of time before the dog gets hit by one vehicle while he is chasing another one.

Solution 1: To break your dog from chasing vehicles, put him in full dress—training collar, check-cord, and e-collar—and use the following procedures:

Walking with the Traffic. Start walking your dog in the same direction the vehicles are going. Use a heavily traveled road that has room for you to walk on the side of it. Be sure you have a good stout check-cord—one he can't break. When a vehicle approaches from behind you and is almost

117

even with you, begin *bumping* your dog with the e-collar using a low level of stimulation. As the vehicle passes him increase the stimulation.

Dogs' reaction to stimulation will vary. Begin with the lowest level of stimulation and move up to the level effective for your dog. Continue this process for several days until your dog tries to get away from the sound of a vehicle approaching from behind.

Walking against the Traffic. Now, change the procedure and begin working him facing the traffic. When a vehicle approaches you, *bump* him with a low setting of the e-collar. As the vehicle passes him, increase the level of stimulation. Continue this process until the dog tries to get away from the sight of approaching vehicles. The dog will associate his discomfort with the vehicle and will try to get away from what he considers to be the source of unpleasantness. Give the dog a two-day rest and then repeat the process to see if he remembers the earlier training sessions and tries to get away from the vehicles. If he doesn't try to get away from the vehicles, continue with the training until he consistently tries to avoid the vehicles.

Testing Your Dog for Anti-vehicle Awareness. Continue the training until you think he is sufficiently afraid of vehicles and then test him. To test the effectiveness of your training, take him to his old chasing ground by the side of a road. Be sure he has his full dress on (training collar, check-cord, and e-collar). When you get to the place where he used to lie in wait for vehicles, drop the check-cord and carefully watch his reactions. If he moves toward a vehicle when it approaches, *bump* him with the e-collar. Increase the intensity of e-collar stimulation so you can stop him if he moves toward the vehicle. If he tries to get away from the vehicle, you know your training has been effective.

Solution 2: For those people who don't have or don't want to use an e-collar, they can use a stick—one that's not too stout—such as a broom handle and use the same procedures outlined above. As a vehicle goes by, give the dog a whack on the shoulder with the broom handle. Be careful. You don't want to whack him in a place that could break a bone.

Chewing or Eating Birds

Problem: A dog goes out to retrieve a bird, but instead of retrieving it he chews on it or eats it. Usually, a handler will yell at the dog trying to stop him from chewing the bird and bring it to him. At this point, many dogs become confused and simply grab the bird, run off with it, and either bury it or eat it. The problem occurs because the handler did not go to the bird with the dog and/or did not keep the training collar, check-cord, and e-collar on the dog when he first started training him in the field. The dog has not been trained to hold the bird and bring it to the handler on command.

Solution: With check-cord in hand, go to the bird with your dog. In this way you can make the correction on the spot.

Never use the e-collar when your dog has a bird in his mouth and is not bringing it back to you. Repeat: You must never use an e-collar on your dog when he has a bird in his mouth. If you use the e-collar on him when he has the bird in his mouth, he'll spit it out unless he has been force broke with the e-collar. That is not what you want him to do. You're giving him a bad signal. You're teaching him to not retrieve. When he has the bird in his mouth, just give a flip of the check-cord to bring him to you.

Usually, he'll bring it back to you—or at least part of the way. Some dogs make good retrievers if you just go to the bird with them a few times without teaching them to hold or force breaking. Your dog has not yet been trained to hold the bird and bring it to you on command. *See* **Chapter 5 – Teaching Retrieving**.

Prevention: If you properly train your dog to retrieve when he is a pup, you will not have this problem.

Collar-Wise

Problem: A dog knows the difference between wearing the e-collar and not wearing it, when he has the e-collar on and when he doesn't. A dog becomes collar-wise when he has had the e-collar put on him only when his handler wants to apply stimulation—not had it on in the last training session where he could chase birds and the handler could not catch him.

It doesn't take a dog long to figure out what the e-collar is when it is put on him only after he has learned to disobey a command. He feels the stimulation only after his handler has used the e-collar to make some training corrections. If he is taken out the next time without the e-collar, he will know he doesn't have it on and will know he'll be able to get away with inappropriate behavior.

Solution: Keep your dog in full dress and condition him to the e-collar. After he is conditioned to the e-collar, remove the training collar and check-cord—but never remove the e-collar. Keep it on him whether you need it or not. *See* **Chapter 3 – Collars, Electronic Collar**.

Prevention: If you keep the e-collar on your dog at all times and properly train with it in conjunction with the training collar and check-cord, he will not become collar-wise.

Cutting Back or Running Behind

Problem: A dog running behind his handler. If a dog has had bad experiences when he is out in front, often he will cut in back of his handler to avoid being reprimanded or scolded. If a dog is running behind 9 o'clock or 3 o'clock from the handler, he is running behind.

Solution: Whether you're training on horseback or on foot, teach your dog to be in front of you—not behind you.

Training on Horseback. If you're on horseback when your dog gets behind you or starts to go behind, call him to you. Get off your horse, pet him, and then give him your signal for going forward. Get on your horse and ride faster to let him know you want him to run in front of you. Continue starting him over until he understands you want him in front of you, not behind you.

Training on Foot. If you're walking, follow the same procedures. After you call him to you, pet him, release him, and then jog with him to give him the idea you will be pleased with him when he is out in front.

Prevention: To prevent your dog from getting behind you, as soon as you see him turn to go behind, stop him right then and follow the procedures given above.

Fear of Horses

Problem: Unfamiliarity with horses—a new experience that frightens the dog. For a dog that has never been around horses, these big animals—knees higher than the dog's back—can be pretty frightening.

Solution: To get your pup accustomed to horses, take him out with a horse and let him run with you and the horse. Of course, use a horse that is accustomed to dogs and will not harm them. Begin by walking the dog as you walk the horse. With both leads—the horse's lead and the dog's lead in the same hand—you can pet your dog while you're walking him. Pet him and then get on the horse so he will get used to seeing you on a horse. He has good feelings about you, and since you are on the horse, he'll associate the horse with you.

Prevention: As soon as you bring your dog home, get him around horses. Get him accustomed to their smell and their size. Pet him when he's around them. Don't let him have a bad experience around horses.

Fear of Water

Problem: Unfamiliarity with water—a new experience that frightens the dog.

Solution: When you discover your dog is afraid of water, get out there with him. Take him swimming. Make it fun. Play games with him in the water. Teach him to retrieve objects. Pet him whenever he does. Water retrieving is a two-fold experience for your dog: He's having fun with you, and he's learning a valuable skill.

Prevention: As soon as you bring your pup home, gradually and sensitively introduce him to water games— anything he enjoys that involves water. Don't throw him into water; it will only make him more afraid.

Fighting

Problem: Dogs will fight for a variety of reasons: to defend themselves if attacked, to protect their young, to chase off strangers in their territory, over their food, over a mate, and so on. Some dogs seem to have an inordinate desire to fight, and some breeds have a tendency to fight more than other breeds. If your dog gets into a fight, the one thing you never want to do is go between two fighting dogs. If you do, one or both of the dogs will probably bite you.

Solution: Methods for breaking dogs from fighting are controversial. One of the most common methods is to spray the fighting dogs with water. Spraying them with a hose may break up the fight, but it doesn't have a long-lasting effect. I don't recommend using a choke chain. A handler attaches a long, strong lead to the choke chain on a dog. When the dog goes for another dog, the handler lets him pick up speed and then bowls him over by sharply jerking the lead.

I have found the best method is using the e-collar. It is the most effective, humane, and long-lasting way. If your dog is aggressive and you want to curb his aggressiveness, put his full dress on him (training collar, check-cord, and e-collar) as you would for training—which is what you're doing. Put him in a situation where he normally fights. When he first shows aggression, use your check cord to vigorously flip the buckle on the training collar and simultaneously *bump* him with stimulation (using more energy than you use during other training). To break a dog from fighting requires more aggressive training than any other type of training. Continue this training until your dog shows no interest in fighting.

Prevention: As you socialize your pup, pay close attention to his attitude toward other dogs. If he's aggressively interested in other dogs, teach him you'll not tolerate it. Break him from fighting as young as possible. It's easier to squelch his fighting tendencies when he is a pup rather than when he is a mature dog. Use the techniques you are comfortable with and the ones you think are appropriate for your dog.

Flagging on Point

Problem: Flagging on point—waving his tail when he's on point—or making other movements such as vibrations that look as if his tail is wagging him. Some dogs are worse than others, but they too can be cured of this annoying problem. It may not be a major problem for you if you're a hunter, but if you're a field trialer, it's a serious problem because you can't win with a flagging dog.

Flagging is normally caused by a handler talking to his dog or sometimes other dogs coming in and taking his birds out, but mostly it is caused by a handler saying *WHOOP, WHOO*, or whatever he says to his dog when he gets around birds. The dog just doesn't know when to stop moving. He's been taught not to flush birds, so he just stands there and waves his tail. He's trying to figure out what his handler is trying to teach him. He doesn't know what the words mean. A dog that flags may have a tendency to creep. Creeping is a more serious problem because the handler is talking to him, and neither of them knows when to stop.

Often a dog will flag if he smells human scent on the bird he's pointing. The bird has human scent on it because it was improperly planted. *See* **Chapter 6 – Using Training Birds**.

Solution: Stop talking to your dog when he is around birds. Approach your dog from the front if possible—at least from some angle where he can see you. Fire your gun into the ground at a good distance in front of him—maybe flushing the bird. Quit talking, and he'll quit flagging.

Prevention: To prevent him from flagging, teach him to *stand-up-stand-still* when you start his field training. Be sure to put pressure on his back and straighten up his head if he has a tendency to *flag*. Be firm in your demands. Insist on his responding to the *stand-up-stand-still* command—always straightening his head so he is looking straight ahead, not to one side. Do more walking. If necessary, put more pressure on his back and hindquarters while you're petting him between birds during the teaching of this command. Talking is probably what caused the problem in the first place. **Do not talk to your dog when he's on point.**

Gun-Shyness

Problem: Fear of loud noises—man-made problem. Any noise that is new to a puppy—such as Fourth of July fireworks, gunfire, a thunderstorm, or someone banging pans on purpose while he is eating—can cause gun-shyness. All too often a handler will take a bird thrower and throw the bird out in front of the pup and fire his gun at the same time. The sound of the thrower will frighten a pup. He doesn't know what causes the noise. It's new to him. Then, to compound the problem, the handler begins shooting over the dog, and this frightens him more.

One couple brought their gun-shy dog to me and asked me if I could help him. I asked them what type of experiences the dog had had around loud noise, and they assured me they had never fired a gun over him. Upon further questioning, I learned the dog had been exposed to a massive fireworks display. When he became frightened, instead of taking him to shelter and comforting him, they tied him to a chair leg on the deck so he could be with them and enjoy the Fourth of July celebration.

Another person brought his gun-shy dog to me. He couldn't understand why his dog was gun-shy. He then explained how he had taken the dog as a pup to a shooting range and hooked him to the bumper of his pickup to get him accustomed to gunfire.

Both of these situations were avoidable. The owners simply did not understand that they were creating the problem.

Solution: *See* **Chapter 7 – Training in the Field, Preventing Gun-Shyness**.

Prevention: Avoid exposing your pup to strange, loud noises. If you can't totally avoid the situation—such as a thunderstorm—try to mitigate the effect by getting him as far away as possible from the noise and by holding and petting him. You may also play a radio near him. Dogs like the sound of a radio, and it diminishes the sound of thunder.

Ignoring Verbal Commands

Problem: A dog does not respond to verbal commands he has already been taught. Excessive and/or inconsistent use of verbal commands can cause confusion and may result in your dog not responding to them because he is not sure what is expected of him. Often a handler will give a command four or five times and then wonder why his dog is not obeying the command he has taught him over and over. He sounds like he's singing a song to his dog. The dog just doesn't know which verse to stop on. Neither understands the command.

Solution: When you give a verbal command, make sure it is a sharp one-syllable word your dog clearly understands and knows what you expect of him when you use it. Be in a position to reinforce the verbal command with whatever method you used when you first taught this command. The watchword as always is consistency. Use each command to mean precisely what you have trained him to respond to. Teach commands over and over until your dog masters them.

The verbal command *WHOA* is commonly used to mean *stop now.* The verbal command *COME* or *HERE* is commonly used to mean *come to me now.* The choice of the word is a matter of personal preference. I prefer the word *here.* It's sharper and carries better, somewhat akin to the word *fore* golfers use to warn people of an errant ball. Use a command that is comfortable for you; just be consistent and use the same one-word command all the time.

Do not add more words such as *come boy, come here, come here ole fellow, good girl, atta boy,* and *come to poppa.* These added words might be causing the problem. When you tack on extra words, your dog may become confused. Dogs twist around when you're talking to them, not because they are happy, but because they're confused— wondering what you want them to do or learn. Dogs can't talk. If your dog doesn't respond to your one-word command, return to early training stages. *See* **Chapter 2 – Starting Your Pup**.

Over Training

Problem: In the training process, the handler has over trained the dog by using too much force or something the dog doesn't understand—such as conflicting and/or confusing commands.

Solution: **Do not talk to your dog except to give specific commands he has learned.** You may solve this problem by shooting a bird for your dog. Go to the bird with him, if he wants to go to it. When the two of you get to the bird, give him a slack check-cord so he can do whatever he wants to do with the bird. He may bring it to you. He may chew on it. He may even eat it. Anything he does with the bird is okay. After he's finished with the bird, pet him and put your happy dog in his crate or whatever you use for hauling him. The session is over for the day.

Pointing Dead

Problem: A dog goes out and points a dead bird instead of retrieving it. The problem may be caused by training your dog to be *steady-to-wing-shot-and-kill* without letting him retrieve, and he's afraid to go out and grab the bird. He thinks the safest thing for him to do is to go out and point it. The problem may also be caused by your dog's inexperience in hunting. He just doesn't know what to do when he finds a dead bird, and he thinks the safest thing to do is point it.

Solution: Both problems are solved the same way. Start him over. Go out and shoot a bird. Take your dog to the bird. Play with him and let him know that it's okay to grab the bird and retrieve it instead of pointing it. Remember to keep the check-cord on him when you take him to the bird so you can control him. Let him have the full length of the check-cord. It's important for you to be able to control him. If not, he may grab the bird and run off with it.

Prevention: Combine the training experience with the pleasurable experience discussed above, and you'll prevent the problem.

Pointing, False

Problem: When clients ask me how to correct a dog for *false pointing*, I tell them their dog is pointing *taints*. Of course, the next question is, "What's a *taint*?" The answer is, "It *tain't* nothing." He may be overcautious and point when there is nothing there; he may point feathers; he may point where a bird has been. When a dog consistently points at nothing, more than likely the problem is the result of the handler talking too much, improper training, over cautioning, or inexperience. If you have over-trained your dog or used too heavy a hand, he'll be overcautious. He's just trying to do what he thinks you want him to do.

Solution: When your dog consistently false points, assume that whenever he goes on point it is a false one. If there is a bird there, pet him after the bird flies to show him that he has pleased you. If there is no bird there (a non-productive), ignore him and continue on your way. Ignoring him and walking away from him shows him you are not pleased with his actions. If he has been trained to go with you, he will leave the non-productive and go with you. After several of these sessions your dog will begin pointing real birds, not imaginary ones.

Prevention: False pointing caused by improper training is usually the result of harshness. A dog that has been treated harshly during his training is afraid, so he points at anything to prevent being chastised. Remember, your dog wants to please you. Never use training techniques that can cause your dog to associate you with his fear or discomfort. False pointing caused by over-cautioning *(ATTA BOY—FIND HIM—GET 'EM—HE'S IN HERE)* is easily corrected. Keep your mouth closed. In fact, keeping your mouth closed solves many training problems. If the false pointing is the result of an inexperienced dog or person, use the solution procedures listed above.

Pointing, Sight

Problem: Sight pointing occurs when a dog points something he sees—not something he scents. This problem, like so many other problems, is the result of improper training—a man-made problem. If you train a puppy to get interested in a fluttering object, such as a bird wing, on the end of a fishing rod it may lead him to point by sight. This early training teaches your dog wrongly. Receiving such training, a puppy will scent a bird and point it but will continue to look around to see if he can spot it.

Solution: Your puppy may look like a champion pointing dog when you're playing with the fluttering object, but he may not point by scent. Take a picture of your puppy pointing. Then put the toy away.

Prevention: Use your fishing rod for fishing—not dog training.

Pottering

Problem: Pottering is similar to false pointing. Instead of pointing, the dog roots around and takes his own sweet time to check out everything in the area. This problem is generally caused by over-cautioning. If he gets the idea you want him to check out everything, this action may become habitual.

Solution: You may correct this problem by scolding your dog verbally. He knows by the tone of your voice you're not happy with him. In addition to scolding him for pottering, use the same techniques you would use for correcting false pointing. Show your displeasure by ignoring him and continuing to hunt. If you're training from horseback, you can get to him quickly. Scold him immediately and get him out of the area.

Prevention: Do not over-caution your dog. Less is best.

Refusing to Hunt with Other Dogs

Problem: A dog refuses to hunt with other dogs when they steal point, flush his birds, and irritate him. Usually, these ill-mannered dogs are young or untrained dogs. Eventually, your dog may get tired of this nonsense and leave to find a place where he can hunt as he was trained to do.

Solution: Hunt him with a well-trained, reliable dog to show he needs to hunt with other dogs. He learns to respect other dogs and they learn to respect him. He learns other dogs will not steal point, not flush his birds, and will honor him. He doesn't have to leave to find better hunting grounds when he is hunting with a dog that, like he, is a good citizen.

Relocating after Pointing

Problem: There are two types of relocation—trainer relocation and dog relocation. Trainer relocation is not a problem. This was something you taught him after he was *steady-to-wing*. The problem occurs when a dog goes on point, relocates himself, and eventually flushes the bird.

Solution: When your dog relocates himself, be at the ready with the e-collar. You have already taught him the e-collar—the most effective correction. Deliver the stimulation to the collar as soon as the bird flushes. Timing is crucial. When he flushes the bird, do not fire your gun. He doesn't deserve to be rewarded for improper behavior. Don't say anything; correct him with e-collar stimulation and spin him.

Use the lowest level possible to stop him—but stop him as soon as the bird comes off the ground. Make the correction immediately. He'll associate the stimulation with either the bird or his own actions. You're still his buddy, and he doesn't associate you with the correction—unless you say something to him. **Do not talk.**

You may also correct him by *spinning* him. To *spin* him, grasp his training collar, raise his front feet just off the ground, and give him a 360-degree spin. If he doesn't have his training collar on, use his ID collar.

Prevention: The prevention lies in the training. *See* **Chapter 7 – Training in the Field, Relocating Your Dog**.

Running Amuck

Problem: After frequent finds, sometimes a dog becomes overly excited. He runs too fast and runs over birds instead of stopping and pointing them. With my type of training, this condition seldom occurs.

Solution: Go back to walking your dog and re-training him. *See* **Chapter 7 – Training in the Field**.

Running at Birds

Problem: Dogs running at birds. People often ask two questions: "When do I stop my dog from running at birds?" and "When do I use the e-collar with my dog when he's on birds?". The latter question might be rephrased, "When do I use the e-collar by itself when my dog is on birds?".

Solution: The answers are simple: (1) Let your dog run at birds until he respects them. *See* **Chapter 7 – Training in the Field, Flying Birds over Your Dog**. (2) When he consistently stops, points, stands, lets you go by him, flush the bird, go back to him, and pet him as the bird flies away, he's ready for you to use the e-collar alone to make future corrections. When you first start using the e-collar alone, turn the stimulation down and leave him in full dress— check-cord, training collar, and e-collar.

Running Away

Problem: A dog runs away from his handler. More often than not, he'll hide from his handler by getting behind something, such as a hill, a clump of brush, trees, or by getting into a ditch. Then, he just up and leaves.

Solution: You simply must start over again. Begin walking him just like you're going to teach him to *stand-up-stand-still*—teach *quartering* and walking on a slack line. If he has not been taught to *stand-up-stand-still*, you'll need to teach him this command.

Work him close to you before you let him get out very far until he indicates he can be trusted. He shows his trustworthiness by turning and coming around to go with you on his own initiative, *quartering*, paying attention to your commands at short range, and gradually getting out farther and farther—still obeying your commands.

Each time you stop him be generous with positive attention (petting). Don't say anything; just pet him. He'll learn to handle. Work with him on the command you use when you want him to pay attention to you, which means you want him to turn and go with you. (I use the word *Hee-YOH*.) You may use this verbal command or one of your choice— just be consistent, and don't use the same word you use for other commands such as *HERE*. Use a different word for each command. Use this command when you're working him close to you, and later you can use it when you are handling him—working him at a greater range. Your dog must thoroughly understand these commands before you give him the liberty of getting too far out.

Running Too Big

Problem: A dog is running too big when he is hunting beyond the range of his hunter or handler or when he's in a field trial stake that requires handling at a closer range.

Solution: *See* **Chapter 4 – Teaching Basic Commands**. Start re-training your dog with the method described in this section. Teach him to hunt, to run, and to handle in the way that meets your needs.

Sitting, Lying, or Dropping on Point

Problem: When a dog sits-on-point, lies-on-point, or drops-on-point, it is a man-made problem resulting from too harsh training or over training. Often when you use the e-collar to *bump* a dog you're in front of, he'll automatically lie down or drop because he doesn't understand what you want him to do. Never *bump* a dog when you're in front of him until he is seasoned on standing and letting you flush. If you start *bumping* him with the e-collar too soon while he's in the breaking stage, he'll be hard to train to *stand-up* when you get in front of him.

Solution: Correct him by teaching him to *stand-up-stand-still* and do more walking. *See* **Chapter 4 – Teaching Basic Commands, Stand-Up-Stand-Still**.

If he has deteriorated beyond this type of training, place the e-collar around his flank. When it's around his flank, put a little pressure on him and force him to sit or drop so you can *bump* him very slightly to see what his reactions are.

Never say anything. Many dogs go berserk when they're *bumped* in the flank with the e-collar. Use minimal stimulation. If he takes the stimulation well, then continue going out in front of him, taking your check-cord with you so you can use it in conjunction with the e-collar to help him stand up if need be.

Patience and caution are the watchwords here. Be patient with your dog. Use stimulation with caution. Be generous with the positive attention (petting), but don't say anything; and you'll be able to correct this problem.

Tracking Bird Planters

Problem: A dog following horse tracks or people tracks is trying to find birds on them instead of trying to locate them by hunting objectives (places where birds are likely to be). In field trials this is considered cheating and will be severely penalized, and rightly so, by knowledgeable and honest judges.

At field trials, people either plant birds in the field being covered by the dogs, or they plant birds in a specific area called a *bird field*. These birds are planted for the dogs to locate and point. Dogs are smart. Some of them figure out if they follow the scent of the bird planter, whether on horseback or foot, they will find birds. This problem is not applicable to hunting dogs.

Solution: To get your dog to stop tracking people or horses during a field trial, stage a training session similar to a field trial. Take your dog to the staged area where birds have been planted on foot as well as from horseback. When you see him begin to track the bird planter—either horse tracks or people's tracks—*bump* him with the e-collar, using no more stimulation than necessary to stop him from tracking.

Continue training until he gets the idea you don't approve of his tracking horses and people to find birds instead of hunting the objectives.

When you get him to where he'll stop tracking when you *bump* him with the e-collar, immediately take him to a place where he can find a bird—not one he's found by tracking a planter or a horse—and shoot it for him. This is his reward. You might also take him hunting, get him into birds, and kill birds for him.

Trailing, Another Dog

Problem: One dog trailing another dog. A dog may trail another dog because he is slower than the other dog, younger, lacks running ability, or he is immature and playful and wants to play. Usually, a puppy who trails another dog to play with him will outgrow this tendency as he gets older and finds other interests while running on his own.

When he gets into birds, he will usually lose interest in trailing another dog. Getting birds is more fun.

Solution: Run a dog that likes to trail with a slower dog. If he continues to trail after you've taught him the e-collar, use it to *bump* him just as he gets up close to the other dog. This *bump* will curtail his desire to trail another dog.

Never bump a dog with an e-collar until you have taught him the feel of it in conjunction with the check-cord and training collar. At the risk of being repetitious, I repeat this warning over and over because it is crucial to my type of training. Using the e-collar without first teaching it in conjunction with the training collar can cause serious problems.

Trailing, Head

Problem: Another type of trailing is called "head-trailing." This type of trailing is more complicated and is seen more often in field trial dogs than in hunting dogs. In fact, you seldom if ever see hunting dogs head-trailing. A head-trailing dog wants to buddy up with another dog. He wants the other dog to follow him and run away with him.

Solution: When you're working with a head-trailing dog, put him with any dog he likes to head-trail and watch him closely. Every time he looks back at the other dog, *bump* him with the e-collar. Remember, you're working with a mature dog that already knows the e-collar; therefore, you can be more aggressive in breaking him of this problem.

CHAPTER 9

MAINTAINING YOUR DOG

Sheltering
Keeping Healthy
Keeping Safe
Conditioning

Providing Shelter

Crate

If your dog is a house dog, the first thing you got for him was probably a crate—the one recommended by airlines. Use this crate for housebreaking your pup, for his bedroom, for his private place during the day, and for his traveling.

If you're using the crate for his indoor doghouse, put in appropriate bedding. Dog beds are readily available in a variety of material. In addition to his crate, if he is a family pet, you may want to get a special dog mat or a blanket you can toss into a corner of a room so he can be with the family after he is housebroken. *See* **Chapter 2 – Starting Your Pup, Socializing Your Puppy**.

Portable Exercise Pen

Folding wire pens are useful in certain instances—when you're traveling and want to get your dog out into fresh air or when you're at a dog show. Your dog can move around but is still controlled. Many people who don't have a fenced yard use these pens to put their puppy or puppies outside in a safe environment. These pens are readily available and come in a variety of sizes. They're basically for short-term use, and you should never leave your dog in them unattended.

Portable exercise pen

Outdoor Shelter

If your dog is an outside dog, you'll need to provide him with a dog run that includes a dog house. It should be warm in cold weather and cool in warm weather. It should be enclosed with wire, and part of it should be covered to provide shade and protection from inclement weather.

The sizes of your dog run and dog house will depend upon the size of your dog. The maximum size of the pen for most bird dogs is 4 feet wide and 12 feet long, with good drainage.

Multi-dog run with houses in back of run

Keeping Your Dog Healthy

Other than you, your veterinarian is your dog's best friend. Choose your vet carefully. You want one you're comfortable with and one in whom you have confidence.

Before you choose a vet, talk to other owners of bird dogs in your area. Ask them about their veterinarian's philosophy and practices. Collect several names of vets; call them and ask if you could have a few minutes interview to help you decide on the vet best suited for you and your dog. Get as many interviews as you can.

When you go to the interview, go armed with a list of questions. Your questions might include the following: Does he or she have a communal waiting room where your dog might be exposed to more illnesses than he brought with him? Will he or she come out to your car to give your puppy his shots? What is the condition of the facility? A brief interview should help you choose a vet that is best for you and your dog. This is a common practice when people are selecting a new physician. If this technique is good enough for people, it's good enough for your dog.

Feeding

The type of food, when to feed, how much to feed, and the type of feeding containers is a matter of preference.

Choosing Food

When you bring your puppy home, continue feeding him the type of food he is accustomed to eating. If you want to switch his food, do it gradually. Feed your dog a good quality food. Some people prefer wet food; some prefer dry food; others—including me—prefer to give dogs both wet and dry food. You may feed your dog raw vegetables—baby carrots, broccoli, cucumbers, and so forth—as treats. Puppies like them, and they provide them with something safe to chew on when they're teething. It's not a good idea to feed your dog raw meat. Check with your vet.

Feeding Schedule

I recommend feeding puppy food to your pup twice a day until he is five or six months old. Then gradually begin switching him to adult dog food—first mixing puppy and adult food. When he is about six months old, begin to feed him adult dog food and feed him only once a day. Some people feed their adult dogs twice a day, and some people prefer to free feed—keep dog food out all the time.

Bowls

Some people use stainless steel food and water bowls, washing them after each use. Others use pottery or glass. There's nothing wrong with using the breakable ones, but if you're traveling or hunting, stainless steel bowls are sturdier and easier to keep germ free.

Emergencies

Your veterinarian will take care of most of your dog's health care needs, but sometimes you may be in a situation where you have to provide first aid for your dog. The following suggestions are based on years of experience with my own dogs and with dogs I train.

First Aid

Whether you are a hunter or a field trialer, you need to keep a canine first aid kit on hand. Your first aid kit should contain the following items: forceps, adhesive tape—various types and sizes—electrolytes, dog thermometer, Ace bandages, tweezers, gauze pads, antibiotic ointment or cream, a couple of 12-inch wooden flat rulers to use as splints, something you can use to muzzle your dog (such as duct tape, bandages, or strips of fabric), and any other items you feel you might need.

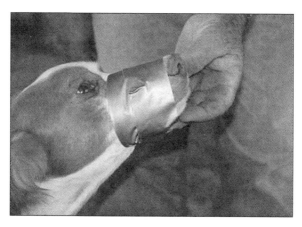

Duct tape muzzle

Broken Bones

If your dog breaks a leg, splint it by taping a board or stick to it to keep it from worsening. Try to keep him calm and get him to a veterinarian as soon as possible. If the broken bone is elsewhere—such as a rib—again try to keep your dog calm and take him to a vet at once.

Choking

If your dog is choking, press his upper lips against his teeth to keep him from biting you. Open his mouth and look at the roof of his mouth and around his teeth and gums. If you find the foreign object, remove it with your fingers. If you don't find anything, pull out his tongue and look down his throat. If you see the object lodged in his throat—and it isn't too far down—use your fingers to remove it. If you can see it, but it's too far to reach with your fingers, use forceps to remove it. If you can't locate the foreign object, get him to the vet as soon as possible.

Superficial Cuts

If your dog cuts his feet when running on rocks and injures his pads, put ointment on the pads and wrap them up. If you're going to continue working in the area, put boots on your dog. *See* this chapter, **Protecting Your Dog's Feet**.

The most common cuts in the field are from barbed wire. If the cut is minor, clean the wound with soap and water and apply an antiseptic cream or ointment, such as you would use on a superficial cut on yourself. If the wound is located in a place you can dress, bandage it using gauze and tape or gauze and an Ace bandage.

Deep Cuts

Hold a compress on the wound to stop the bleeding and take him immediately to a veterinarian.

Dislocations

If you notice one of your dog's joints is swollen and he is carrying the limb at an unnatural angle, he has probably dislocated the joint. Put a muzzle on him to keep him from biting you, apply cold compresses, and take him to a veterinarian. Do not delay. Any delay may affect the resetting of the joint.

Heat Strokes

Heat stroke is the most serious problem hunters and trialers have in the field. In hot weather do not work your dog in an area where there is no water available. Before you plan to work in an area unfamiliar to you, check it out. Locate water sources so if you need water, you'll know where to find it. If there is no water and you're determined to work the area, carry water with you to keep your dog watered. Water him frequently.

When you think your dog may be over-heated, take immediate action. When a dog is overheated, he will appear dazed or unable to stand and have difficulty breathing. Cool him as quickly as possible. Look for a stream, a spring, a watering trough, or any place where you can get him into the water.

Keep him in the water until his body temperature returns to normal and his breathing is no longer labored. More than likely, he'll try to get out of the water, but don't let him out until you're completely sure he is no longer in danger.

When he can swallow give him electrolytes (a liquid bottled form commonly found in grocery stores such as Pedialyte or Gatorade) by pulling out his lip to form a pouch and pour the electrolytes into the pouch so that it can drain into his throat. **Do not pour water or any other liquid directly down your dog's throat.**

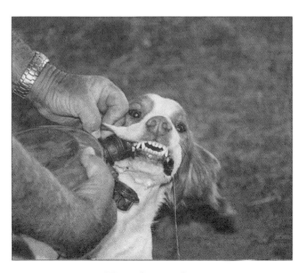

Watering a dog

Internal Bleeding

If your dog is listless and unable to stand or walk after having an accident, he may be bleeding internally. Don't take a chance. Keep him as calm as possible and get him to a veterinarian immediately. Internal bleeding is a life or death situation.

Motion Sickness

Often dogs suffer from motion sick while riding in a vehicle or flying in a plane. Usually, they get car sick because they're not accustomed to riding in a vehicle. Take your dog for short trips and get him used to riding. Usually, he will stop getting car sick. If your dog continues to get sick after several trips, ask your veterinarian for anti-motion sickness medication.

Puncture Wounds

Puncture wounds are usually the result of a dog fight. Don't try to care for this type of wound yourself. Take him to a veterinarian.

Shock

Dogs, like people, can go into shock after an extreme fright or a serious injury. Symptoms may include weakness, thirst, nausea, labored breathing, and in severe cases, unconsciousness. If you think your dog may be in shock, do not allow him to move. Keep him calm. Keep him covered to keep his temperature constant. Get him to a veterinarian as soon as possible.

Sprains

Sprains are much like broken bones. The area will be tender and swollen. Try to keep your dog calm and still, and, if possible, use a splint. Take him to a veterinarian at once.

External Parasites

Some excellent medications are available for preventing or getting rid of external parasites—ticks, fleas, and lice. Check with your vet for recommendations for the best and most appropriate medications for your part of the country.

Ticks

If you're working your dog in an area that may be tick infested, be sure you check your dog for them—especially under his collar, under his forelegs, around his ears, and between his shoulders.

If you find a tick, use tweezers or forceps, grasp the tick as closely as possible to the skin and with a firm but steady pull, slowly remove it. Don't touch the tick. Kill it by placing it in alcohol. The head of the tick should come out with the body. Whether it comes out or not, cleanse the wound with alcohol twice a day for several days. In this way you can prevent the wound from scabbing and permit it to drain. If the area where the tick was imbedded becomes swollen or your dog develops a fever, take him to your vet immediately.

Internal Parasites

When you bring your dog home, have him checked for worms. Call your vet, and, more than likely, he or she will ask you to bring a stool sample when you take your dog in for an examination. Your veterinarian will tell you what you are supposed to do for the various types of intestinal worms as well as heart worms.

Grass Awns

These slender bristle-like appendages are found on the spikelets of many grasses—notably cheat grass, foxtail, and spear grass. These prickly little burs are a nuisance when they get into your socks or shoes, but they can be more than an annoyance to your dog.

If you're in an area where your dog may pick up awns—usually in his ears or feet—check him often and carefully remove these potentially dangerous burs. If you don't, they can burrow into the skin and move into the tissue. If this happens they have to be surgically removed.

Do's and Don'ts

Do keep your dog in your vehicle until your vet is ready to see him and then take him directly into the examining room—not into a common waiting room.

Do ask your veterinarian to come out to your vehicle to give your dog a shot—particularly a puppy—and thus not expose him to the host of airborne diseases—including parvo which has over 20 different strains—he could be exposed to in the office.

Don't expose your dog to other sick animals in a common waiting room at your vet's office.

Don't use kerosene or gasoline to remove paint or tar from your dog's coat.

Don't use kerosene or gasoline to kill lice and ticks on your dog.

Don't use a lighted cigarette or match to remove ticks from you dog's skin.

Safety

If you're planning to hunt or work your dog on private property, first get permission. Before you hunt the area, find out if there are any traps, snares, poison, or conditions potentially dangerous for your dog. If the area isn't safe, don't put your dog in harm's way. Find another place.

If you're hunting or working your dog on government land (land where many field trials are held), the government posts the area if snares, traps, poison, and so forth exist.

Snake Bites

If you hunt or train your dog in an area that has poisonous snakes, you may want to consider taking your dog to a trainer who is experienced in snake breaking dogs.

A new vaccine is now available. *See* **Appendix 4 – Useful Names and Addresses**. A dog needs two initial shots and a booster shot every six months or 30 days before possible exposure. If you're going to run your dog in snake country, plan ahead. It takes 30 to 60 days for a dog to build up required antibodies after the initial vaccination. Check with your vet. Even after your dog has been inoculated, you still must take him to your vet for further treatment if he is bitten.

Feet Protection

When you're hunting in an area that can be hazardous to your dog's feet—rocky terrain, rough sandy areas, and stickers—protect your dog's feet with dog boots. There are several different kinds including canvas, rubber, and leather. I prefer rubber ones. They look something like the covers of golf club irons. Most of the time I just put the boots on the front feet—unless the stickers are really bad—because a dog carries about 65 percent of his weight on his front feet.

Boots come in different sizes. Choose ones that fit your dog. The way you put the boots on the dog is important. First wrap your dog's leg with medical tape. Put the boot on and turn one side of it down and tape the other side to the dog's leg. Next turn the other side up and tape the two sides together. In this way you will have no holes in the boots that sand or other debris can get in, and the boots will stay on your dog's foot.

Note: Lewis Dog Boots of Enid, Oklahoma, makes good boots. *See* **Appendix 4 – Useful Names and Addresses**.

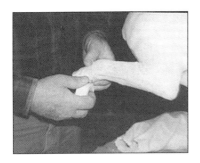

Taping dog's foot

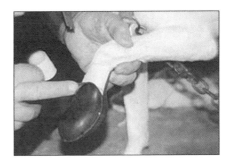

Boot fitted over taped foot

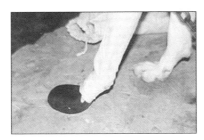

Foot taped, boot top folded and taped to foot

Finding Your Lost Dog

When you lose your dog, whether you're hunting or field trialing, the best way to hunt for him is the way you lost him. If you were walking when you lost him, he'll probably back track your scent and be at your vehicle when you return to it. If he's not there when you get back, wait for him as long as you can.

If you were on horseback when you lost him, hunt him on horseback. He'll be just as concerned as you are and will try to find you by tracking your horse.

If you can't find your dog and you have to leave the area, be sure you leave an article of your clothing with your scent on it—a shirt, sweater, or jacket. The clothing will let him know you haven't forgotten or abandoned him, and he'll stay there with the piece of clothing until you return.

There is really no need to lose a dog nowadays with all the modern electronic tracking devices available.

Conditioning Your Dog

Condition your dog in two ways—by *running* him and by *roading* him. You *run* him by taking him to a field and hunting birds. You *road* him by attaching him to a moving vehicle or horse and having him pull against resistance. Your dog is an athlete, and, like any other athlete, he must be in top-notch condition if he's going to perform at his maximum potential.

If you're a hunter, don't wait until right before hunting season opens to get your dog in shape. If you do, don't expect to have anything at the end of the day except a tired, worn-out dog unable to hunt the way you hoped he would.

If you are a field trialer, don't wait until just before the competition and expect your dog to bring home any ribbons.

Keep your dog conditioned year-around. Whether you're conditioning your dog for field trialing or for hunting there is no substitute for running. In the summer time you may not be able to run your dog due to environmental conditions. Beware of lack of water, hot weather, or snakes which are especially hazardous in certain parts of the country, particularly the Deep South and Southwest. However, when possible, *run* and *road* about 50/50 percent of the conditioning time.

Watering Your Dog

Know your dog. Some dogs tend to be lazy and are not strong pullers. Other dogs are aggressive pullers. When you begin roading a dog that has not been conditioned, make sure you don't overheat him. Water him down to reduce his body temperature. Put a barrel of water (or more if you're roading more than two dogs) in an area where you can go to it (or between them if you have several barrels out) as you need to put your dog into water to cool him off. Stop your dog every few minutes to cool him down.

Dogs being cooled and watered in water barrels

Caution: Always *read* your dog. Don't let him get overheated. Be aware of the weather conditions and his condition. Carry a canteen of water with you. If you think your dog may be over-heated—tongue lolling out and panting excessively—water him. Different trainers water their dogs in different ways. Some water their dogs using the cup from their canteen. Others pull out the dog's lip so it forms a pocket and pour water into the pocket. Use whatever system works for you. Just be sure you water him when he needs it. **DO NOT pour water or other liquid down your dog's throat.**

Roading Your Dog

If your dog is young and/or has never been *roaded*, you must first teach him how to *road*. You will need a roading harness (available from Cabela's, Dunn's, and other suppliers). Put a roading harness on him. At first attach a check-cord to his ID collar and put weights on the roading harness. If you just attach the dog to the roading harness, he doesn't know what to do and will start turning around rather than pulling.

When he becomes accustomed to pulling, attach the check-cord to his roading harness instead of his ID collar. Continue to use weights if he doesn't pull against the roading harness without the weights attached.

Conditioning weights and harness

A roading harness is similar to a sled dog harness. It has a ring on each side to which you can attach weights. Take a rope, long enough to clear your dog's legs when he is pulling, and fasten a snap on one end of the rope. Fasten the other end to the chain with a clamp. You will use the fastener to attach the weights which will provide resistance training when your dog is walking or pulling. Put equal weights on both sides. An athlete doesn't train just one side of his body. He conditions his whole body. Likewise, you want to develop the muscles equally on both sides of your dog.

Four dogs in roading harness attached to ATV bar

Conditioning Weights

Adjust the weights on your dog according to his size, condition, and temperament. You may use 20-pound weights on some dogs and 5 pounds on others. As your dog gets into shape, you can add more weight. The snaps on the rope make it more convenient to change the weights.

Walk your dog on the check-cord until he is comfortable walking with the weight of the check-cord and the attached weights. When you begin roading him from horseback, ATV, or whatever vehicle you're using, he'll not be scared because he'll know how to pull to condition himself because he has already adjusted to pulling weight.

Protecting Your Dog's Legs

When you put weights on a dog, be sure the fasteners on the rope attached to the weights don't chafe his legs. Be sure the rope is long enough for the fasteners to clear his legs when he is pulling and long enough to keep the weights behind his back legs. Adjust the length of the rope to the size of the dog. Obviously, bigger dogs take longer pieces of rope than smaller ones. One way to keep from hurting or injuring your dog with the fastener or the rope is to encase the rope and fastener in a plastic tube. (Garden hose or possibly PVC pipe will work.)

When you start roading your dog, it's a good idea to road him every day, if possible. You may use a vehicle or horse to road him. Sometimes when I'm on the road field trialing, I have to use a horse for roading dogs; but, when I can, I use a 4-wheeler.

Roading several dogs from an ATV

Caution: Don't rode your dog on a bicycle unless you have a roading bar long enough to keep the dog away from the bicycle. Don't road your dog on a bicycle using only a check-cord. This is a dangerous practice for both you and your dog. *See* **Appendix 1 – Grooming and Showing Your Dog, Roading on a Bicycle**.

To use a vehicle, put your dog in a roading harness and attach the harness to a roading bar attached to your vehicle—all terrain vehicle, jeep, truck, car, or sled. Roading bars come in many shapes and sizes. The one you use will be determined by your preference and the number of dogs you will be roading. If you're roading your dog from horseback, attach the check-cord to the roading harness, keeping the check-cord in your hand. **Never** tie the check-cord to your saddle. If you do and your horse runs away, your dog will probably be killed.

Roading a dog from horseback

After dogs are conditioned to pull against the roading harness, many of them will no longer need weights. They are highly motivated and will pull hard without the weights. This is what you want. Some dogs are less motivated to pull and will always require weights.

When you road your dog, road him at a speed where he'll be pulling in a stress situation—resistance exercise. Train your dog just like athletes train. Pull for a while, sprint for a minute or so, and then stop. Check your dog.

When you first start roading for the season, watch your dog closely. Be aware of weather conditions. Be attuned to your dog. Remember a dog wants to run, and some will run till they die. You're responsible for *reading* your dog. Is he panting too hard? Is his tongue lolling out? Does he need watering? You don't want your dog to suffer a heat stroke.

Roading Several Dogs

When you road several dogs at a time, be sure you have all the dogs with you ready to be harnessed and hitched to the roading bar so you don't have to leave them unattended while you're going back to get other dogs. If left unattended they can get into fights because some dogs don't like to have another dog alongside them.

If you're roading two rows of dogs, put the dogs needing the most conditioning in the back row and attach weights to them. Don't put weights on the front dogs. If you do, the dogs behind them will step on the weights.

Appendix 1

Grooming and Showing Your Dog

By Fay Walker

Bathing
Brushing
Cleaning
Preparing to Show

Basic Grooming

Begin grooming your dog as soon as you bring him home. If you have a grooming table, that's great, but if you don't, try to do most of the grooming on a sturdy table. Picnic tables work fine. You'll need a grooming table hook—available at dog shows, pet supply stores, or various catalogs advertising dog equipment and supplies. An adjustable table suitable for your height is ideal. The table not only makes it more comfortable for you, but it gets him accustomed to being touched while he's on a table—good training for those necessary visits to the vet.

Puppy fastened to hook on grooming table

It's best to start with ten-week old puppies since they submit easily to table training. Older dogs may be a little more challenging and struggle with being hooked up snugly. If a dog wants to sit while you're working on the front, that's okay. To work on the rear end, place your hand between his back legs and give the verbal command *STAND*. In this way you can work on the tail and hind legs with clippers and thinning shears.

Pet him, handle his paws, examine his toenails, move your hands gently over his body. Make it fun. In this way you'll get him used to being handled on a table. Then, when you need to check his body—especially eyes, ears, legs, and between toes—for foreign particles, to brush or comb him, to trim his coat, to cut his toenails, and so forth, his cooperation will make life easier for both you.

Caution: Don't leave your dog unattended on the grooming table. It is a dangerous situation and can result in your dog's death because he may try to jump down thereby hanging himself since he is still attached to the hook on the table.

Bathing Your Dog

Do not bathe your dog too often. You shouldn't bathe your puppy before he is three or four months old—unless you absolutely have to. A good rule of thumb is to bathe him when he needs it—when he smells less than wonderful, when he is really dirty, or when you're going to show him. Use a pH 5 shampoo for general bathing. For removing grease or diesel fuel from his coat, use liquid Dawn™ dishwashing detergent. Use a good conditioner such as Mane and Tail™ or a salon formula you would use on your hair. It will make your dog's coat more luxuriant and remove dryness from the skin (dandruff).

Your dog's coat is his insulation blanket—the means of keeping heat in or keeping it out. When you bathe him, you are temporarily removing the body oils from his insulation blanket. Make the bath as comfortable as possible for him: Use water that's close to his body temperature—about 100 degrees.

After bathing him, allow him to shake excess water off and dry him well with a towel. You may use a hair dryer to finish drying him, although a hair dryer tends to dry out the hair making it look dull. Dogs tend to roll after they've had a bath, so it's a good idea to keep them inside until they're completely dry. This is particularly important for a puppy because exposure to outside elements could cause him to catch a cold.

The weather and your part of the country will determine whether you can bathe your dog outside. In the summertime when the weather is extremely warm, you can take your dog outside and bathe him using a garden hose and letting him air dry naturally. Outside bathing produces an excellent sheen to his coat, but, of course, you can only do this when the weather permits.

Caring for Your Dog's Coat

Use a brush, a comb, and, if necessary, a shedding blade to care for your dog's coat. During the shedding season, use the shedding blade to remove excess hair. Shedding blades are available at pet stores.

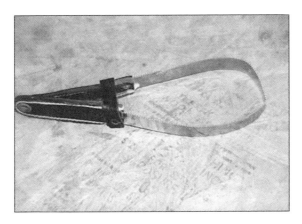

Shedding blade

When in dire straits, if you don't have a shedding blade or can't find it, use a hacksaw blade. To remove bits of dirt, seeds, burs, and so forth from most long-haired sporting dogs, use a comb. In addition to removing these bits of debris, fine-toothed combs will remove lice and fleas. Brush him often to distribute the hair oil which will keep his coat healthy and give it a nice sheen. If your dog's hair gets matted under his ears and between the legs, use scissors or clippers to remove the mats or hairballs.

Checking Your Dog's Ears

Periodically check your dog's ears. Clip any hair which might impede the flow of air into the external auditory canal. Check for mites or infections. If the ear canal is inflamed or smells bad, first clean the ears with a good ear cleaner such as R-7™—available from your vet or in catalogs that cater to dogs' needs. After you apply the cleaner, let your dog shake his head—and he will—then wipe out his ears with a soft damp cloth, using only your forefinger. In this way you can remove any foreign substance or bodies. Repeat as needed.

Dr. Scholl's™ foot powder is a time-honored remedy for ear mites. Just put the powder in a squeeze bottle and dust his ears with it. To clear up infections, use Otomax®, which may be purchased at a veterinary clinic. If the problem persists take your dog to the vet.

Removing Unwanted Debris

When your dog has been in the field, always check him carefully and remove any seeds or burs from all parts of his body. You can make your life and his much easier if you practice an ounce of prevention. Hint: Apply mineral oil to your dog's coat before he goes into the field or just spray his coat thoroughly with Pam™ or a generic substitute. The main ingredient in most cooking sprays is Canola oil. Both products work well and are easily removed with soap and warm water. Applying either of these products makes it easier to comb out foreign particles—briars, cockleburs, sand spurs, seeds, and so forth.

On female dogs you can spray them using the can, but with male dogs you should only spray the forefront—not the rear end. Be sure you do not get any spray in your dog's eyes or nose.

Be very careful when you use the spray on a male dog. You do not want to get any of the spray on his testicles—it can cause sterility. To apply the spray to his hindquarters, spray a cloth or your hands with the product and apply it carefully, avoiding the testicles.

Caring for Your Dog's Toenails

Start clipping your dog's nails early—as early as three weeks. Use pocket nail clippers at first. You want to get him accustomed to this grooming. It is this aspect of grooming that dogs dislike most and one that is frequently neglected by owners. Use the nail clippers until your dog is about two months old.

How to Trim Toenails. Whether you are trimming the toenails of a puppy or a mature dog, use the same process. If you're right handed, start with the left hind foot. If you're left handed, start with the right hind foot. You begin on the hind feet because dogs do not object as much to work on their hind feet as they do on their front feet. By the time you get to the front feet, the dog has begun to get accustomed to the grooming, and your task is made easier.

Take one of his toes between your thumb and forefinger with his paw resting in the palm of your hand. Look at the toenail. Part of it will be clear, except for black nails. This is where you will clip or grind the nail. You must use good judgment. The quick is the part that is not clear. If you clip or grind too closely to the quick (a little white visible area)—and sometimes you will—you will hit it. Don't panic if he bleeds; apply a powdered substance called Kwik-Stop® that stops the flow of the blood. This product is readily available at pet stores, dog shows, and from pet supply catalogs. Many people use powdered coffee creamer if they don't have Kwik-Stop®.

If you're using a grinder such as Oster® or Dremel®, buff the nails after you have finished—rounding them so they are smooth. To keep your dog's nails looking good, healthy, and to prevent breaking, give him a pedicure about once a month. Many dogs intensely dislike the clippers but will tolerate grinders. To them it seems to be the less of two evils.

You may purchase grinder with a stone or with sandpaper. I find the stone is better because it lasts longer. Choose the type that best meets your needs. Battery operated grinders are available.

Cleaning Your Dog's Teeth

You can frequently get a scraper (periodontal spoon) from your dentist—one that has been damaged and no longer can be used on human beings. They're usually free. Hold the scraper between your thumb and forefinger and scrape downward on the incisors (the top long, fang-like teeth). Place your thumb to the back of his teeth and scale the molars, chipping plaque downward so as not to injure the gums. The bottom teeth do not build up plaque like the upper teeth do but can be scaled chipping upwards.

After scaling your dog's teeth, brush them using a soft brush and a pre-brushing mouthwash such as Plax™. For some reason or other, my dogs prefer the red Plax™. You may want to use canine toothpaste if you brush your dog's teeth often. Gently hold your dog's mouth closed and work the brush up and down—brushing both the teeth and the gums. You can usually keep your dog's teeth and gums clean and healthy by scaling once a month and brushing once a week. If you have the time and are so inclined, you may brush them more often.

Between cleaning sessions, buy your dog a large beef bone from your butcher—that is if you have only one dog. Chewing on the bone will help keep his teeth naturally clean. If you have more than one dog, the bone can create problems. Even the gentlest dogs may fight over a nice meaty bone. Some dog owners give their dogs large-sized Nylabones® as an alternative to real beef bones. These synthetic bones do not seem to trigger the hostility the beef bones do.

Purging Anal Glands

Many dog owners prefer to leave the task of purging anal glands to their veterinarian. If, however, you want to perform this necessary procedure yourself, it is relatively easy. The anal glands are located on either side of the dog's anus. Bring up the tail and with your forefinger and thumb feel for the gland, which will feel full to your fingers if the glands need to be purged. Gently squeeze the glands to expunge the fluid. Be careful. The fluid can spray in any direction. Keep your head at a safe distance and to the side. Continue pressing on the glands to be sure they're empty. After you've finished, cleanse the area with a damp cloth. For visual step-by-step instructions, see my video *The Dual Dog,* **Appendix 4 – Useful Names and Addresses, Dog Training Videos**.

When your puppy is about four weeks old, his anal glands need to be purged. A puppy gives no indication this needs to be done, but an older dog will scoot his rear on the carpet or ground. Some people think this action indicates the dog has worms. This is not usually the case; rather his anal glands are probably full.

Not only is this procedure necessary for your dog's health, it also contributes to his carrying his tail erect and looking more stylish.

Showing Your Dog

If you decide to show your dog yourself and have never done so, find a local kennel club that puts on conformation classes. These classes will teach you how to show your dog to the best advantage. It is fun for both you and your dog. You will get many good ideas and have the pleasure of seeing other breeds. You will learn about the availability of clubs and seminars pertinent to showing.

Preliminary Training

Before you take a conformation class, begin some preliminary work at home. If your dog is still a young puppy, get a good show collar and lead—available at dog shows and from some pet supply catalogs—and begin practicing in your yard. Some show collars and leads are all in one.

Walking Your Puppy

Start with walking and get him accustomed to walking on a lead. The lead should be light nylon or leather for showing (not a 6 foot or check-cord type of lead). If your puppy is not responding to this training, you might want to switch to a training collar and a check-cord. This training may take two or three days of consistent work—about 15 minutes twice a day works well.

When he is walking well wearing the training collar and check-cord, switch back to the show collar and lead. You want to get your puppy accustomed to walking on a lead and turning and going with you. When pivoting, form a clicking sound with your tongue or your mouth— whichever works for you and your dog. Your dog will become accustomed to the sound, and when you pivot, the clicking will be a cue to turn. The turn will become a flowing motion making the dog look elegant on a loose lead.

Trotting Your Dog

As he consistently walks with you, slowly work him up to a trot because this is the gait you'll be required to use in the show ring. If you don't do this preliminary training, your puppy will not know what to do when you take him to his first match or accredited show.

Standing for Examination (Presentation)

After he is comfortably trotting with you, you're ready to move him to another phase of his preliminary training—getting him to stand for examination. It's best to start this training with him on a table. To teach your puppy to stand for examination, place his front legs straight under his shoulder, using your left hand place his hind legs backwards at a slight angle. After you have him standing still, use both hands with an upward motion stroking under his chin and tail. This stroking encourages him to look his best for presentation. At this point you may bait—feed him a morsel of food he likes, such as cooked liver, chicken, or wieners—to keep him focused while the judge examines him. Some judges forbid baiting, but others do not.

Taking a Conformation Class

Conformation entails the judging of the size, proportion of the body, substance, and height of a breed. After you've worked with your pup at home, and he is responding nicely, now is the time to get in touch with your local kennel club to find out if conformation classes are being offered. Both you and your pup will benefit from these classes. You'll have more information, be more confident with your puppy, and have a better idea of what is needed to show your dog. While you learn, your pup too will learn. This is his initiation into the dual dog world.

Taking Your Dog to His First Match

After you've taught your dog to walk, trot, and stand for presentation, The All Breed Match (put on by local kennel clubs prior to the big show—something like a practice run) is a good place to formally start your pup.

If you have a great dog you think has potential in the show ring, but you have neither the time nor interest in actually doing the showing yourself, then you will probably want to find a professional handler who will show your potential champion.

Fay (third from left) and her Brittany show champions

Conditioning Your Dog

Conditioning show dogs differs from conditioning field dogs, but some aspects are similar. When you're planning to enter your dog in a show, you should do some conditioning at least a month or so before the show and during the show. Judges have begun to seriously consider the condition of show dogs—in addition to their conformation and style.

If you have an ATV set up for conditioning field dogs, great. This is an ideal situation, but if you have a horse, bicycle, scooter, or are a jogger or walker, you can still do the job. In all five roading situations, use a roading harness. If you're roading from an ATV, you'll need a roading bar and a roading harness. For a more complete discussion of conditioning, *see* **Chapter 9 – Maintaining Your Dog, Conditioning Your Dog**.

Roading on Horseback. If you're roading your dog from horseback, in addition to the roading harness you'll need a long check-cord—about 20 feet.

Roading on a Bicycle. If you're roading your dog from a bicycle, in addition to the roading harness or ID collar, you'll need a Springer™ (a device that attaches to the back wheel of your bicycle). This device can be purchased at dog shows or from a catalog catering to canine needs. It provides the dog with resistance pulling while he is trotting alongside you. In addition to providing resistance pulling, it prevents the dog from getting under or in front of your bicycle. Using the bicycle and the Springer™ is an excellent way of training at the show grounds. It's more convenient than an ATV or horse.

Note: Electric scooters are currently all the rage.

Roading on Foot. If you're a jogger or walker you can condition yourself while you're conditioning your dog. You'll need a roading harness and a shorter check-cord— about 12 feet—and a good pair of walking or jogging shoes. Attach the check-cord to your dog's roading harness and tie the other end around your waist. Walk or jog—depending on your preference—for about two miles every day before the show and during the show.

Appendix 2

Scenting

Dogs have incredible scenting ability. They live in a world of scent. Generally, the average dog's sensitivity to smell has been rated from one hundred to a million times greater than that of an average human being. They not only have a natural keen scenting ability, this ability can be enhanced by training. Through their phenomenal sense of smell, dogs have been guarding, protecting, and feeding their owners for ages. Following are a few exotic ways dogs help their human companions: hunting truffles; discovering avalanche and earthquake victims; tracking escapees; sniffing out bombs; detecting hidden illegal drugs such as marijuana, cocaine, and heroin; detecting the difference between fraternal and maternal twins; and detecting certain types of illness.

Recommended Reading

Case, Linda P. *The Dog: Its Behavior, Nutrition and Health*, 2nd Ed., Blackwell Publishing, Ames, IA. (2005).

Greenlee, Martha H. 2004. "Scent: A Discussion of Game Birds and Bird Dogs." *Field Trial Magazine*. Volume Eight, Issue Three, Summer 2004.

Greenlee interviewed fellow game bird hunters Dr. Michael Siegel and Dr. Timothy Smith. Based on the information she derived from the interview wrote this informative and provocative article. For people interested in understanding scenting, good scenting conditions, poor scenting conditions, factors affecting scenting, kinds of scenting, and changing scenting conditions, this article is a must read.

Martha H. Greenlee—sculptress of note, outstanding amateur Brittany breeder, trainer, hunter, field trialer, and writer—with Dave Webb, co-authored

The Brittany: Amateurs Training with Professionals, Glade Run Press, Valencia, Pennsylvania, 2003.

Dr. Michael Siegel—physical anthropologist and professor—Department of Anthropology and Orthodontics, Associate Director for Research of the Cleft Palate-Crainofacial Center University of Pittsburgh.

Dr. Timothy Smith—associate professor, School of Physical Therapy, Slippery Rock University, adjunct research associate professor, Department of Anthropology, University of Pittsburgh.

Dr. Siegel and Dr. Smith are currently conducting research on the Vomeronasal Organ (Jacobsons Organ).

Pollard, H.B.C. *The Mystery of Scent.* London: Eyre and Spottiswoode, 1937. A classic book on scent.

Smith II, Charles. Excerpt from Hunting Diary.

Based on data from hunting records that include high temperature, low temperature, wind direction, wind speed, percent relative humidity, dew point, specific humidity, coveys found, number of birds in each covey, Smith developed a formula for choosing good days for scheduling hunts.

On the best days, the specific humidity ranged from 92 to 138 grains of moisture per pound of dry air. The Trane Air Conditioning Manual defines specific humidity as being humidity ratio, which is the weight of water vapor mixed with one pound of dry air—7,000 grains equals 1 pound. The amount of specific humidity is calculated with a psychrometric chart and knowing the dry bulb temperature (the one TV weather people refer to) and the relative humidity. Find where these two intersect on the chart and then read across to the right in a straight line to the specific humidity scale.

In the case of south Texas, if we want to get "Texas" analytical with scheduling our hunts on the best days for the dogs' scenting abilities to be most effective, we schedule our hunts on days when the wind is blowing from 8 to 25 mph; temperatures ranging from 42°F to 85°F, with relative humidity levels between 55 and 95 percent.

Wind speed did not seem to be a factor in the dogs' scenting ability. A major factor in the dogs getting a lock on the bird (dead or alive) was (1) the amount of chlorophyll in the vegetation, and (2) the citric acid in the citrus orchards along with the ground moisture from irrigation.

In talking with Bert Tumey of B & D Game Farm in Harrah, Oklahoma, he shed some light on the role weather plays in scenting conditions: "The quail (as well as other game birds) has a preening gland that produces oil. The bird uses it to oil its feathers during damp or wet conditions in order to keep itself dry. The bird runs its beak across the gland and then applies the oil to its feathers, thereby distributing the scent."

In conclusion, the heavier the air (high specific humidity), the wetter the air, the more likely the bird is going to preen thus giving off more scent and making for better scenting conditions. In field trials, it's not uncommon for seasoned trialers to ask bird planters if they're wetting down the birds before releasing them along the field trial course or planting them in the bird field. Conclusion: A wet bird is more likely to preen and spread the scent to its feathers than a dry bird.

Smith has shown dogs professionally for many years, has his own kennel, and is an avid field trialer and hunter.

Appendix 3

The Beaufort Scale

The Beaufort Scale—a scale of wind force—was devised by Admiral Sir Francis Beaufort (1774-1857) of the British navy. Successive ranges of wind velocities are assigned code numbers from 0 (calm) to 12 (hurricane), corresponding to wind speeds of from less than 1 mile per hour to over 74 miles per hour. An adaptation of this scale is used by the U. S. National Weather Service.

Force	Name	Effect on Land	Wind Speed mph
0	Calm	Smoke rises vertically	Less than 1
1	Light air	Weather vanes inactive; smoke drifts with air	1 – 3
2	Light breeze	Weather vanes active; wind felt on the face; leaves rustle	4 - 7
3	Gentle breeze	Leaves and small twigs move; light flags extend	8 - 12
4	Moderate breeze	Small branches sway; dust and loose paper blow about	13 - 18
5	Fresh breeze	Small trees sway; waves break on inland waters	19 - 24
6	Strong breeze	Large branches sway; umbrellas are difficult to use	25 - 31
7	Moderate gale or Near gale		32 - 38
8	Fresh gale		39 – 46
9	Strong gale		47 – 54
10	Whole gale		55 – 63
11	Storm or Violent storm		64 – 74
12	Hurricane		Greater than 74

Appendix 4

Useful Names and Addresses

ELECTRONIC COLLARS

Tracker Radio Location System
774A Purtle AV
Springdale, AR 72764
479-751-5119
800-900-2113
www.trackerradio.com
The New Tracker Classic®
Bark Collars

Tri-tronics
1705 S. Research Loop
P. O. Box 17660
Tucson, AZ 85731
1-800-456-4343
tritronics.com
support@tritronics.com
Electronic collars
Only e-collar recommended
by Dave Walker

Wildlife Materials Int.
800-842-4537
1202 Walnut Street
Murphysboro, IL 62966
www.wildlifematerials.com
Recovery Collar®
The one used by Dave Walker

DOG AND TACK SUPPLIES

Cabela's
One Cabela Drive
Sidney, NB 69160
www.clubs.akc.org/brit
www.cabelas.com

Dog Boots
580-237-1292
P. O. Box 10572
Enid, OK 73706
Protective Dog Boots

Dunn's Sporting Goods
P. O. Box 189 AF
Grand Junction, TN 38039
713-764-2041
Toll Free: 888-456-5150

Jeffers Pet
P. O. Box 100
Dothan, AL 36302-0100
1-800-jeffers (533-3377)

Lion Country Supply
800-622-5205
www.LCSupply.com

Red Rock Biologics
P. O. Box 8630
Woodland, CA 95776
Toll free: 866-897-7625
Fax: 866-575-7625
www.redrockbiologics.com
info@redrockbiologics.com
Snake bite vaccine

Rocksteady Supplies
R.D 2, Box 341D
Saltsburg, PA 15681
1-800-354-8964
rockstdy@kiski.net

Tarpin Hill Saddle Co.
1650 North Broadway
Salem, IL 62881
1-800-354-8964
618-548-8942
www.tarpinhil.net

Trail Blazin' Innovations (TBI)
8711 Belle Glen
Houston, TX 77099
1-281-530-3916
www.TBICatalog.com

Walker Plantation & Kennel
3615 Cassia Road
New Plymouth, ID 83655
208-278-5074
www.davewalkerdogs.com
davewalker@aol.com
*Dave Walker Training Collars,
Check-cords, and Training
Videos and DVDs:*
**Puppies Started Right
The Finished Dog,
Using the Electric Collar
Meat on the Table
The Field Trial Dog
Teaching Your Horse
 to Ground Tie
Correcting Problem Dogs
How to Ground Tie
The Dual Dog** by Fay Walker
Teaching Labs to Point and
Snake Proofing Your Dog
 by Bill West

ORGANIZATIONS

American Brittany Club
P. O. Box 616
Marshfield, MO 65706
www.clubs.akc.org/brit

American Field
542 South Dearborn St.
Chicago, IL 60605
312-663-9797

American Kennel Club
919-233-9767
www.akc.org

National Dog Registry
P. O. Box 116
Woodstock, NY 12498
Tel 914-679-Bell
Fax 914-679-4538
800 NDR-DOGS

Glossary of Terms

aggression—The practice or habit of launching attacks on other dogs or people.

all-age dog—A classification in field trialing—a big running, bold, independent dog with lots of class that shows reasonable handling.

Amateur Field Champion (AFC)—The title a field trial dog earns when he has earned 10 points in a licensed AKC trial with an amateur handler. *See Field Trial Rules and Standard Procedure for Pointing Breeds* put out by the American Kennel Club, Inc.

backing—*See* honoring.

bark collar—A battery powered collar that automatically delivers a low level of stimulation to the dog's throat when he barks.

bird dog—A dog used to hunt game birds.

bird launcher—A device for putting birds into the air for training purposes.

birdless—A dog that has found no birds during a given event.

bird thrower—*See* bird launcher.

bird-wise dog—A dog that recognizes a liberated bird—one that he can catch.

bird work—Any work a dog does involving birds—whether it is good or bad.

bird work, good—A dog pointing a bird and standing there until his handler arrives.

birdy—Body movement indicating the presence of game.

bitch—A female dog.

blinking birds—A dog scents a bird, turns, and leaves.

bloodline—The history of a dog's breeding. *See* pedigree.

bold dog—A dog that confidently approaches and points a bird he has scented. Generally, a bold dog is more easily trained than a non-bold dog.

bolt—To run away. A bolting dog will take off in any situation.

brace—Two dogs.

broke dog—A dog that stands through the *wing-shot-and-kill* sequence and remains standing until his handler releases him.

broke-to-wing—*See steady-to-wing.*

broke-to-wing-and-shot—*See steady-to-wing-and-shot.*

broke-to-wing-shot-and-kill—*See steady-to-wing-shot-and-kill.*

broke-to-wing-shot-kill-and-retrieve—See steady-to-wing-shot-kill-and-retrieve.

bump **with e-collar**—To deliver a level of electronic stimulation.

bump **with foot**—Gently tap a dog's hocks with the side of the foot.

bumping birds—A dog finding a bird and continuing to move causing the bird to flush.

busting birds—*See* bumping birds.

call-bird—A bird that is usually left in a call-back pen to call back birds that have been released.

call-back pen—The pen to which the birds return after being released.

canine hip dysphasia (CHD)—A disease affecting a dog's hind legs.

cat-walking—A dog that goes on point and continues to move. Also called *creeping*.

Champion (CH)—The title a show dog earns when he earns 15 points with 2 majors.

check-cord—A rope, about 9/16 inch diameter no more than 12 feet long with a snap at one end.

check-cording—Using a check-cord by itself to walk a dog. Using it in conjunction with a training collar to teach commands and to get the dog accustomed to the feel of each one. Using it in conjunction with the training collar and an e-collar to get him accustomed to the feel of the e-collar.

cutting back—A dog running behind 9 o'clock or 3 o'clock from the handler. Also called *running behind*.

dam—Pedigree term for a dog's female parent.

DEAD—Hunt a dead bird—one dog did not see fall.

dog—Male dog.

dropping on point—A dog dropping down when he should be on point.

edges—Transitional zones such as fence rows, ditches, and so forth—a line of cover.

electronic collar—A battery powered stimulation collar used to teach and reinforce commands. Also called an electric collar or an e-collar.

establishing point—A dog adopting a pointing stance.

FETCH—A verbal command given by a handler to a dog to tell him to go, get a bird, and bring it back.

fetch—Retrieving an object or a bird. The performance of the dog in responding to the command *FETCH*.

FETCH—The command given to a dog to get him to open his mouth.

fetch-to-hand—A dog fetching a bird and holding it in his mouth and delivering it to the hand of his trainer on command.

Field Champion (FC)—The title a dog earns when he has won 10 points under the point rating schedule as outlined in *Field Trial Rules and Standard Procedures for Pointing Breeds*, The American Kennel Club, Inc.

field trial—Dog competition in the field.

field trialer—A participant in a field trial.

flair collar—A brightly colored or iridescent dog collar that makes the dog more visible at a distance or at night.

flush—To rouse and cause to move or to fly off.

flushing—A bird being flushed by anything—a dog, car, person, etc. When a dog goes on point, his handler will go into the area and attempt to flush the bird. He is said to be flushing whether there is a bird there or not.

force breaking—*See* force retrieving.

force retrieving—Using force to train a dog to retrieve.

full dress—A training collar, a check-cord, and e-collar worn by a dog during training.

game bird—A bird, such as quail and pheasant, hunted mainly for sport, especially a bird protected by game laws.

GIVE—A verbal command to a dog to release a retrieved object in the trainer's hand—often used in teaching force retrieving.

good citizen—A dog that obeys the commands of his trainer, as a person is a good citizen who obeys the laws of his or her society.

green-broke—Partially broke—not seasoned.

grouse—Any one of various plump, chicken-like game birds hunted from coast to coast, usually in wooded areas.

gun-shy—Fear of some loud noises caused by improper exposure.

hacking—A handler constantly calling to his dog.

handle—Working with a dog in the field—teaching him to respond to commands.

handling—A dog responding to commands he has been taught.

hard mouth—The mouth of a dog that bites or chews birds.

heart worms—A worm transmitted to dogs by mosquito bites.

head-trailing—A dog that is constantly running in front of other dogs.

Heinz 57 dog—A dog of mixed breeding.

HERE—The verbal command given to a dog to come to the person who gives the command.

honoring—Staying clear of another dog on point and honoring the pointing dog by looking like he too is on point.

horse shy—Fear of horses caused by lack of exposure.

HUNT DEAD—*See* DEAD.

identification collar (ID)—Usually a name tag with pertinent information on a collar a dog wears at all times.

johnny house—A house in which birds are kept for training dogs.

liberated bird—A bird deliberately let loose for the purpose of training, hunting, or increasing the population.

loose lead—A slack lead or check-cord.

lying down on point—*See* dropping on point.

making game—Body language of the dog showing he smells birds.

marking a bird—A dog watching a bird and marking where it lands when shot or when it flies to another location.

nonproductive—A dog pointing at something other than a bird—possibly some animal or a place where a bird has been.

objectives—Places where birds are likely to be.

OFA—Orthopedic Foundation for Animals.

patterning—A dog hunting where the hunter or trainer wants him to hunt, also called *quartering*.

pedigree—Certified purebred for several generations.

people shy—Fear of people.

petting—A physical form of praise for a dog to reward him for correct responses. Stroking the dog with the tips of the fingers—moving from front to back, also called *stroking*.

pigeon—A non-game bird used for dog training.

point—A dog scenting a bird, freezing, and his body becoming rigid—*goes on point.*

pottering—Dawdling—a dog rooting around investigating everything he encounters.

purebred—Belonging to a recognized breed established by breeding dogs of unmixed lineage over many generations.

quail—An extremely popular chicken-like game bird—includes several varieties.

quartering—*See* patterning.

range—The distance between the dog and his handler.

recall pen—*See* call-back pen.

registered—A dog with a registration certificate affirming its breed.

releasing a dog—Using a tap, a whistle, or a verbal command to give a dog permission to continue hunting.

relocating a dog—Giving a dog permission to move and re-establish point after he has been released.

respect birds—A dog respects birds when he demonstrates he recognizes they have the ability to cause him discomfort. Example: A prize fighter respects another fighter when he knows the other fighter may be able to beat him.

roading—Conditioning by pulling against resistance—using a roading harness—working the dog from a vehicle, horseback, or on foot.

roading harness—Collar type device to be placed around a dog's chest and belly—same as used to harness sled dogs.

running at birds—A dog trying to catch a bird by chasing it.

running away—*See* bolt.

running behind—A dog running behind his handler (9 o'clock or 3 o'clock).

running big—Term used in field trials for all age dogs, also called handling.

running too big—Hunting out of the range of his hunter or handler or when he is running a field trial stake requiring handling at a closer range.

running wide—Running the maximum range the terrain allows.

running trash—Hunting or chasing anything other than game birds.

sage hen—*See* grouse.

sensitive dog—A dog that responds better to rewards than punishment.

singing—The *singing* or *yodeling* a field trialer does to stay in touch with his dog to give him directions and commands. Different handlers use different sounds. Some sound like they're calling a ball game; some like they're on the opera stage; and others like they're selling peanuts, popcorn, and crackerjacks.

sire—Pedigree term for a dog's male parent.

sitting on point—A dog sitting down when he is on point instead of standing rigidly.

spinning a dog—A disciplinary action performed by grasping a dog's collar, lifting his front legs just off the ground—enough to enable him to pivot on his back legs—and giving him a 360-degree spin.

sporting breeds—Pointers, setters, spaniels, and retrievers.

stake—A specific field trial event.

stake-out chain—A chain or cable with stakes at each end and short lengths of chains with snaps spaced at appropriate intervals on the chain for securing one or more dogs.

stand-a-bird—When a dog points a bird and stands on point until his handler arrives.

stand-up-stand-still—A non-verbal command for the dog to stand up and stand still—used while training for being *steady-to-wing*.

steady-to-wing—A dog that stands and lets his handler flush the bird and does not move until his handler releases him.

steady-to-wing-and-shot—A dog that stands and lets his handler flush a bird and fire over him—not killing the bird—and doesn't move until his handler releases him.

steady-to-wing-shot-and-kill—A dog that stands and lets his handler shoot a bird—killing it—and not moving until his handler releases him.

steady-to-wing-shot-kill-and-retrieve—A dog that is steady through the *wing-shot-and-kill* sequence and does not move until his handler sends him to retrieve the bird.

stealing point—Instead of honoring another dog's point, the dog moves in front of the other dog and either chases or points the bird.

STOP—*See WHOA.*

stone-broke—An expression that implies that a dog is 100 percent reliable in the *wing-shot-and-kill* sequence.

stroking—*See* petting.

stop-to-flush—A game bird flushes in a dog's presence and the dog stops and remains standing until his handler releases him.

stud dog—*See* dog.

taking out a bird—*See* bumping birds.

tether—A string by which a bird's foot is fastened to a piece of cardboard so as to limit the distance the bird can fly but does not tire the bird as does a weight or heavier object.

trailing a dog—A dog consistently following or running alongside another dog.

trailing a bird planter—Dogs that hunt for birds by following the scent tracks of a bird planter on foot or the scent tracks of a horse the bird planter is riding—a field trial problem.

training collar—A collar used for starting dogs in the training process.

trash—*See* running trash.

WHOA—A verbal command used to stop a dog. The dog's appropriate response to the command is to stop and stand still until released.

woodcock—Either of two types of related game birds having brownish plumage, short legs, and a long bill—commonly called a *timber doodle.*

yard work—Dog training when a dog is under control in a controlled environment.

Index

H

I

J

L

M

N

O

P

Quick Order Form

☎**Telephone orders:** Call 208-278-5074.

💻**email orders:** www.davewalkerdogs.com

📧**Postal orders:** Wade & Moeur Publishing, LLC, Dave Walker, P.O. Box 623, Ontario, OR 97914, USA.

Please send the following books, CDs, audio tapes, videos, DVDs, training collars, or check-cords. See our website www.davewalkerdogs.com for a complete product list or call 208-278-5074.

_____

_____

_____

_____

Please send more FREE information on:
❑ Seminars
❑ Presentations
❑ Mailing Lists
❑ Training

Name: _____

Address: _____

City: _____ State: _____ Zip: _____

email address: _____

Phone: _____

Sales tax: Please add appropriate percent for products shipped to your address.